Edwin Charles Clark

Early Roman Law

The Regal Period

Edwin Charles Clark

Early Roman Law
The Regal Period

ISBN/EAN: 9783744774758

Printed in Europe, USA, Canada, Australia, Japan

Cover: Foto ©Suzi / pixelio.de

More available books at **www.hansebooks.com**

EARLY ROMAN LAW.

THE REGAL PERIOD.

BY

E. C. CLARK, M.A.

OF LINCOLN'S INN, BARRISTER-AT-LAW,
LECTURER IN LAW
AND LATE FELLOW OF TRINITY COLLEGE, CAMBRIDGE.

London:
MACMILLAN AND CO.
1872.

INTRODUCTION.

THE beginnings of Roman law are only noticed incidentally by Gaius or his paraphrasers under Iustinian. They are, however, so important and at the same time so difficult a subject that the attempt to set forth what is known or may be inferred about them, in a continuous form, needs no apology. With the execution of the task I fear it may be different: and a crossfire from jurists and historians might not unreasonably assail an encroacher on the debateable ground between the two provinces. Still, a careful collection of the best known original authorities on early Roman law may not be without use, even though the theory should prove erroneous upon which, as framework, our scattered fragments of knowledge are put together. From one source of error—the retailing of quotations—I trust this book will be found free. Most of the passages cited have been arrived at by independent reading of the original authority: the few others have been carefully verified.

As regards *scope*, it was my intention to have included the Twelve Tables: but I have found the subject of the Regal Period, little as we know of it, to require so much reading that I am obliged to postpone the Decemviral legislation to a time of greater leisure. There must, however, occur here, as a matter of course, many detached references to a code which was in great part merely a collection of previous laws or customs.

The *method* which I have adopted has been to furnish, as far as possible, in the text of each section, a tolerably continuous account of the subject in hand, relegating quotations and references to the notes. For those readers who may wish to acquire any substantial knowledge of the subject I need not mention that here, as

> Au Perse de Casaubon,
> La sauce vaut mieux que le poisson,

the fish being my own, the sauce that of Varro and Festus.

In the matter of *orthography* I must apologize for certain inconsistencies. In all *continuous* Latin I have adopted the principle of making no symbolic distinction between the palatal vowel (I) and palatal spirant (sometimes written J), or between the labial vowel (U) and labial spirant often written V). Such a distinction I believe to be not only destitute of good authority, but misleading. I should have preferred to employ the same symbol for the capital as for the small writing, both of labial and palatal: but V capital and u small seem too firmly established in good modern editions for me to disturb them.

Where *detached* Latin words occur, particularly in the text as distinguished from the notes, I have felt a great difficulty and ultimately moved in a strange diagonal which may possibly please no one.

With words docked of their terminations, which therefore may fairly be regarded as naturalized English, I came at once to the conclusion that it was best to spell them in the usual English manner altogether. Vergil for Virgil or Ouid for Ovid seem to me as bad as Livorn would be for Leghorn or Firence for Florence. But where a word has been taken unchanged, except in the symbol for vowel or spirant, the matter is not so simple. I must here plead guilty to the weakness of retaining our English form of very familiar words such as Nerva, Juno, Servius, Flavius, decemvir, &c.

The *spelling* is intended to be that of the Ciceronian period.

The *dates* are those of the *city* (A.V.C.) according to Zumpt's *Annales*. Where an event is not mentioned in that chronology, its date is here fixed by reference to the consulship under which it happened and the year given by Zumpt for that consulship.

The only *references* which do not speak for themselves are those to Corssen's Aussprache, Vokalismus, und Betonung, in which the *pageing* of the second edition, and those to Ortolan's Explication Historique des Instituts, in which the numbering by sections of the eighth edition, is followed. To the interesting and valuable work last mentioned I may here testify my very deep obligation.

CONTENTS.

EARLY ROMAN LAW.

REGAL PERIOD.

§ 1.

SOURCES. ORIGINAL DOCUMENTS. IUS PAPIRIANUM.

IT is scarcely necessary to say that no *original documents* of legislation during the regal period at Rome have come down to us. Assuming that the early laws were reduced to writing and were even engraved on oak, as we are told by Dionysius of Halicarnassus, we could not expect that much survived the destruction of Rome by the Gauls. In fact, Livy expressly states that the military tribunes of the following year (v.c. 365) ordered all the treaties and laws which were in existence to be sought out, and that these last were the Twelve Tables and *some* laws of the kings[a].

Nor are we more fortunate in the possession of *copies*, at least in any regular and perfect form. What seems to have been the only collection of regal law known to Romans of the literary period was mythical in its origin and perhaps also limited in its scope. Sextus Pomponius asserts all the laws introduced by the kings to have been extant at the time when he wrote, in a collection made by Papirius, a contemporary of the last king[b]. Pomponius,

whose Enchiridion is preserved in the first book of the
Digest (Tit. 2. 2.), appears to have written in the time
of Hadrian (870—891 v.c.), whom he styles **optimus,**
but not, as he does Hadrian's near predecessor **Nerva,**
diuos[c]. The book to which he refers was called, it seems,
ius ciuile Papirianum—the collection or body of law
edited by Papirius. It has been pointed out[d] that the
form, or title at any rate, of *ius*—a *body* of law—is later
than the regal period. Individual laws were probably
entered, as they were enacted, in those commentaries of
the pontiffs which appear to have been the first Roman
records: a code, for the times to which it is attributed, is
an anachronism both in a philosophical and literary point
of view. Some of the pontifical records may have escaped
the general conflagration, others would be re-written from
memory. Out of these, in later times, a collection was
probably made and dignified with the name of some legendary celebrity—perhaps originating in a real personage
—whether the Gaius Papirius who collects Numa's laws
after the expulsion of the kings, the Manius who becomes
the first *rex sacrorum*[e], Pomponius' Publius who collects
the royal laws, or the Sextus of the same authority who
contrives to exist in the times of 'Superbus the son of
Demaratus the Corinthian'[f].

The *source* here ascribed to the *ius Papirianum* tallies
with a brief indication of its *contents* given by Servius the
commentator on Virgil. 'The poet,' says he, 'in the expression *morem ritusque sacrorum* has used the very title
of the *lex Papiria*, which he knew was published on the
subject of ceremonial ritual[g].' Against a *lex* Papiria of
early times there is not the same objection, in point of
anachronism, as against a *ius* Papirianum: though the
term would more naturally mean a statute carried under
Papirius' auspices (compare our 'Lord St Leonards' Act,'

'Locke King's Act,' &c.) than a statute edited by Papirius. The ambiguous word *publicatam* adds to the difficulty. Its most proper meaning is *divulged*, of something before kept secret. Now it is worth remark that Pomponius makes Publius Papirius the instructor in law of Appius Claudius the Decemvir, proceeding directly afterwards to mention Appius Claudius the great reformer, who made public the Potitian rites[h], and, through his dependent Flavius, the grand pontifical secret of the fasti[i]. May it have been possible that the so-called Papirian law was the work either directly or indirectly of the latter of these two early Claudii, whose true political character is conclusively shewn by Mommsen[k]? If there should be any truth in this suggestion, it is quite conceivable that even the aspiring Gn. Flavius, who dared to let the newer *legis actiones* come forth under his own name, might yet think it wise to seek an ancient title for the more revered though less important relics of royal times[l]. Zumpt argues from the term *lex* that there were several subdivisions of the *ius* Papirianum, to one only of which Servius here refers[d]. Mackeldey considers *lex* to be used for *ius*, and the whole work to have been confined to religious matters[m].

The supposition of the former author is very probable, that the Papirian collection, whatever its antecedents or contents, was mainly known to our authorities by the edition of Granius Flaccus, who wrote under Caesar's dictatorship[n]. To this source we should refer the fragment cited by Macrobius as part of the *ius Papirianum*[o]; and from this, rather than from any remains of the original pontifical books, is most probably derived all that we know of regal legislation.

---

a. Livy, 6. 1. foedera et leges—erant autem eae XII tabulae et quaedam regiae leges—conquiri quae comparerent iusserunt.

b. Digest. 1. 2. 2. **§ 2.**

c. ib. §§ 32. 47.

d. Zumpt, Criminal-recht, Abach. 1. c. 3 and Anmerkk.

e. Dionysius Antiqq. **3.** 36: **5. 1.**

f. Digest. 1. 2. 2. §§ 2. 36.

g. **Servius** on Virg. Aen. 12. 836, quod ait (Vergilius) *morem ritusque sacrorum* ipso titulo legis Papiriae usus **est quam sciebat de ritu sacrorum publicatam.** The passage **does not appear in all editions,** **e.g.** the Basle Virgil **of 1561.**

h. **Livy,** 9. 29.

i. id. 9. 46.

k. **See the** masterly Appendix to Vol. **1 of his History.**

l. Livy, 9. **46.** Digest. **1. 2. 2. § 7. Cicero de Orat. 22. i. 41. 186.**

m. Lehrbuch des Römischen Rechts, § 21 Anmerk. f.

n. Paulus in Digest. 50. 16. 144.

o. Macrob. Saturno. **3. 11. See too Heineccius Antiqq. Prooem. 2. not. c.** I scarcely understand Schöll's condemnation of Wesseling, **Dirksen and Schwegler,** who, he says, attribute this fragment to **Granius Flaccus 'without any sufficient reason.'** All that can be **meant by them is that the passage in question** (beginning 'ut in **templo' inquit 'Iunonis Populoniae augusta** mensa est') is no **original document, but the illustration of a comparatively** recent **writer, who is perhaps more likely to have been Granius** Flaccus **than any one else. See, however, Schöll. Legis XII Tabb. Reliqq. p. 51. n. 3.**

§ 2.

SOURCES. HISTORIANS, JURISTS, ANTIQUARIANS.

IN the absence either of original documents or full copies, we must fall back in the first place upon such *quotations* as bear evidence of at least high antiquity and are reputed fragments of regal legislation. It need scarcely be said that professed imitations, such as those in Cicero's treatise de Legibus, must be entirely excluded except as evidence of the views received in the imitator's time. Even reputed quotations must be looked on with suspicion when they shew traces of comparatively modern phraseology. The mere attribution, however, of a fragment of legislation evidently old, to a fabulous or half-fabulous author should not invalidate the fragment itself, but is rather useful as giving us a traditional *date*, which may be correct, if not absolutely, at least relatively to other fragments. We may, for instance, disbelieve the very existence of Romulus, Numa or Tullus, but if we find three fragments attributed respectively to these three personages, we shall not, perhaps, be wrong in believing that there was at least some real ground for the fragments being placed at a very remote period and in a certain order of time.

As a secondary source of our knowledge on the present subject I regard the *statements* made by ancient authors about the first beginnings of Roman law. This latter source, though more plentiful, must be considered far inferior in purity to the former. Had they even possessed the means, writers of antiquity rarely possessed the inclination for the close critical enquiry into early history which has only reached its full developement in very modern times. It may seem strange to place our *means* so high in comparison with theirs, when so many works on history and antiquities have totally perished and others have only reached us in a mutilated condition. But, fragmentary as our authorities are, it must be remembered that they extend over the *whole* period of ancient intellectual activity, so that we have, at least in this respect, an advantage over all but the very latest ancient writers. In all points, too, connected with words or phrases which were obsolete at the Greek or Roman literary period, we are aided by the entirely modern science of comparative philology; while, with the ancients, the false derivations and spurious antiques which this knowledge enables us to detect, undoubtedly led to much erroneous speculation and possibly to some garbling of facts.

The inclination for critical enquiry seems generally to have been stronger in Greek than in Roman writers. It is very evident in Herodotus, Thucydides and Polybius, and more so, as it seems to me, in the despised Dionysius than in Livy. But in neither of the last two writers—our principal authorities for early Roman history—is it at all strong in comparison with a contrary tendency from which neither historians nor jurists have ever been free; I mean that of unconsciously attributing the principles and procedure of the writer's period to the men of an earlier day: a tendency which, while at some times it will merely produce anachronous detail in an account mainly true, will at others give rise to stories of institution and enactment entirely false. We have the more harmless result in those picturesque touches which make Livy so charming and those speeches and sermons which make Dionysius so dull: the more dangerous one is to be feared in constitutional history proper, to which the latter author devotes much more attention than the former. The above remarks of course apply not merely to the regal period but *mutatis mutandis* to the whole history of the Roman law. For the early republic, in fact, while we have more information, we have also very evidently a new source of error in the unfair and exaggerated family records from which our historians have probably in great part drawn their accounts*. In this very respect, however, any connected history stands higher than biography proper, which is, beyond question, the least trustworthy of authorities. There is much less scruple in attributing exploits of peace or war to the hero in hand when his life stands to a certain extent detached, than when it has to be woven into a continuous account, the parts of which must be respectably consistent. From the classical *jurists* we should have expected fuller and more trustworthy records of ancient legislation than we actually find. They, however, wrote mainly for present practice; and, as the old law had been to a great extent superseded by what we may roughly call equitable modifications, the references to the former are occasional and slight. Moreover the theory of a law of nature, which entered so largely into their conception of a *ius gentium*, was not perhaps entirely without influence upon their treatment of the *ius ciuile;* it being probably found more agreeable and easy to connect even their old national law with supposed original principles of morality than with actual ancient customs or records. Still we owe a great deal of valuable information upon the present subject to Gaius and the Digest, though more perhaps to other sources.

It is on the *antiquarians* that our principal reliance must be placed: a class of men with whom form is of greater importance than matter, who quote rather than paraphrase, who are more interested to preserve an ancient relic intact, than to make a picturesque story, to develope a moral theory, or to glorify a noble family. In the note to this section a brief account is given of our principal authorities of this kind, as of the too little known Dionysius[b]. Since the works of these authors, though extremely interesting, do not seem to come much in the way of ordinary readers, the necessary quotations from them will generally be given, in the notes, somewhat fully.

a. This fact has long been recognised in the case of Livy. It is almost equally clear with Dionysius. See, inter alia, his reference to certain τιμητικά ὑπομνήματα, which were evidently *private family histories.* Antiqq. 1. 74.

b. Dionysius of Halicarnassus. Wrote his Ρωμαϊκή Ἀρχαιολογία during the 22 years following his arrival in Italy, which seems to have been shortly after the battle of Actium. See Antiqq. (Antiquitates Romanae, the Latin style of his work under which it will be hereafter referred to) 1. 7. καταπλεύσας εἰς Ἰταλίαν ἅμα τοῦ καταλυθῆναι τὸν ἐμφύλιον πόλεμον ὑπὸ τοῦ Σεβαστοῦ Καίσαρος, κ.τ.λ.

Zumpt (Criminal-recht der Römischen Republik, Einleitung, p. 9) allows this author much more credit than is usually given him. Dionysius had, no doubt, as he tells us, read all the histories extant in his time, as well as accumulated much information from private family records. Being a faithful reporter of legends, many of which have some literary, though little historical, value, he is not, except in the article of speeches, quite such dreary reading as has been represented by Lord Macaulay and others. He does not impress one as often guilty of direct invention; but his small critical power and consequent inability to sift his materials according to their value, and his inveterate tendency to moralize, render him undoubtedly an untrustworthy authority. It is in the regal and first republican period that this tendency appears the most: so much so that at times we might almost suppose ourselves to be reading a Télémaque of less inventive power than Fenelon's but about the same historical value. It was perhaps a similar despair of a decayed society felt by pureminded and conscientious men which disposed both authors to attribute so much to the heroic worthies of half-fabulous times.

Of Livy of course I need say nothing but that he wrote after the triumph of Augustus, A.V.C. 725 (as appears from 1. 19. of his history), and died according to Eusebius A.V.C. 770.

Festus (Sextus Pompeius), the epitomizer, writing in the 2nd or 3rd century after Christ, of a lost work 'on the signification of words' by M. Verrius Flaccus, an author of Augustus' time. Flaccus is mentioned by Varro (see below), quoted in Macrobius' Saturnalia, 1. 15, 21, as iuris pontificii peritissimum. This Epitome is only known to us by the still briefer one of Paulus made in the 9th century, which appears to have supplanted the original, and by a fragmentary copy of the latter, now in the library at Naples. There seems, however, no reason to think either of the editors of Flaccus' work disposed (or perhaps qualified) to tamper with the fragments of old Latin, which may therefore be regarded as genuine antiques, or at least so considered in the time of Augustus. Of our two sources, the Naples fragment is evidently the

more valuable as far as it goes: Paulus occasionally substituting
the views of Festus for those of Flaccus without remark. Thus,
we read in the fragment, *Sas* Verrius putat significare eas...cum
suas magis uideatur significare. Paulus, who quotes the same
authority for the meaning (a passage of Ennius), writes at once
sas suas. On the next word, *sam,* he retains the error 'philoso-
phiam,' though he omits the words 'sapientia quae perhibetur,'
which point to the right reading:—

nec quisquam sophiam sapientia quae perhibetur
in somnis uidit prius quam sam discere coepit.

From these and similar instances one would conclude that
Paulus represents Festus pretty faithfully, and when he misrepre-
sents him does so only by way of omission. As to Festus himself,
the frequent 'Verrius putat' of the fragment certainly shews a
conscientious reproduction of the original even when the epitomizer does not agree with it. I have used the edition of Müller.

Varro (M. Terentius) a Pompeian, after the battle of Pharsalus
taken into favour by Caesar, and devoting his life thenceforth to
laborious study. See Cicero, Ep. ad fam. 9. 6. ad Atticum, 13. 12.
His proscription and escape from it, under the second triumvirate,
as well as the voluminousness of his works, appear from a quotation by Aulus Gellius, Noctes Atticae, 3. 10. in which Varro mentions his having attained a twelfth hebdomad of years and written
seventy hebdomads of books, many of which had disappeared on
the pillage of his library after he was proscribed. It is the extant
part of his treatise de lingua Latina, which is most cited in the
present work. Whether this treatise was sent (dedicated) to
Cicero, and therefore completed before 711 v.c., is not certain,
though Müller apparently thinks it probable. See Praefatio ed.
1833. I have used his edition.

Aulus Gellius, the author of the well-known Attic Nights, was
when young a pupil of Fronto (who was Consul Suffectus A.V.C.
896 in the reign of Antoninus Pius) N. A. 19. 8. He is supposed
to have died before 917 v. c. Many valuable records of legal
antiquity are to be found in his work, particularly in the last
(20th) book.

Servius Maurus Honoratus, the Commentator on Virgil, is
introduced by Macrobius (Sat. 1. 2. 15) as an interlocutor with
Symmachus, Consul under Theodosius and Valentinian, A.V.
1144, and the well-known champion of the old religion against
Ambrose. In the gathering of *Savans* which forms the subject of
the Saturnalia, Vettius Praetextatus is the first host, who would
appear from an inscription to have died A.V.C. 1140. Servius

is represented in the above-cited passage of Macrobius to have recently come forth as a critic, when the supposed social gathering took place; which statement, coupled with the 'charming modesty' which is there attributed to him as well as 'wonderful learning,' will perhaps justify us in considering him to have been a man of middle age about the end of the 4th century of our era. Many interpolations are supposed to have been made in his commentary, but there is no mistaking the tone of the principal writer in it, by which one may tell with some confidence whether a particular note has the Servian ring or not: I mean the extraordinary talent for finding obscure and mystical meanings in the plainest passages, to which a perfect modern parallel is furnished by Landino's commentary on Dante. A specimen occurring early in the Eclogues is so exquisitely amusing that I may perhaps be pardoned for adding it below. However, the desire of Servius to make every incident and epithet in Virgil emblematic of some old Roman custom or belief has preserved to us a most valuable and interesting body of antiquities.

On Ecl. 3. 96, 97 he writes:- *Tityre pascentes a flumine reice capellas*, id est, O Mantua, noli modo nolle aliquid agere de repetendis agris, nam cum opportunum fuerit *ego omnes lauabo* id est purgabo apud Caesarem cum de Actiaco proelio reuersus fuerit, et bene *in fonte*, ipse enim per amicos Caesaris agrum meruerat recipere tanquam per riuulos quosdam, nunc autem Mantuanus beneficium dicit se ab ipso Imperatore meriturum.

Of *Macrobius Ambrosius Theodosius*, if that was his name, the author of the most interesting ancient work on antiquities extant, we know little but that he must have lived at least not before Praetextatus and Symmachus, whom he introduces in his Saturnalia. He seems to have been *Consularis*, a title which in late times did not necessarily imply the bearer to have been Consul, as indeed Macrobius' name does not appear in the Fasti. This honour, however, conferred upon a man who can scarcely have embraced the new faith, is well urged by L. Iahn (Prolegg. v.) as a reason for not placing Macrobius much later than the interlocutors in his supposed dialogue.

§ 3.

ORIGIN, CUSTOM.

THE late Mr Austin, in his Province of Jurisprudence, lays considerable stress upon the correct apprehension of the term *customary law* in its strict sense: in the sense, namely, of a rule which has at some time been set, either directly or indirectly, by a political superior, whatever be the anterior circumstances by which the rule has been suggested or its enactment rendered possible[a]. The soundness of this view is beyond question as far as regards the law proper of an established and regularly constituted state. It might, however, give rise to an error (from which the writer in question is doubtless free) as to the *historical* origin of the earliest laws in infant communities. In many cases these laws, improperly so called according to Mr Austin, appear to have existed as rules of conduct dependent upon custom, long prior to any official enactment[b]. Individual legislators have indeed been assigned or invented for the oldest rules which have descended to us, whether they have actually remained in the form of custom or been re-cast in the mould of law. Thus Dionysius makes Romulus institute the *patria potestas*, the relation of patron and client, &c.[c]: and the fragments which Verrius Flaccus has preserved are attributed by him, or his compiler, to Romulus and Tatius, to Numa, to Servius. But we have a surer guarantee than these venerable names, for the antiquity of a custom, in the evident deduction from it of historical constitutional usages, and for that of a fragment, in its own language, viewed by the light of comparative philology. For full information on the latter head, reference must

be made to the labours of Corssen and Mommsen; but
a compendious and accessible collection of early Latin is
also contained in the late Dr Donaldson's interesting
Varronianus[d]. We are here concerned less with form,
except as evidence of antiquity, than with matter;
from a consideration of which it would appear that
the earliest Roman 'laws' were embodiments of *custom*, generally bearing a religious or quasi-religious
character, and often referring specially to that system of
the *family* common to all infant states, yet nowhere
attaining such wide developement and lasting influence
as at Rome.

a. Austin's Jurisprudence, Lect. 1. pp. 103—5, ed. 1869.
b. See Maine's Ancient Law, ch. i. pp. 7, 8.
c. Antiqq. 2. 10. 26, 27.
d. Specially Corssen's Bei- und Nach-träge zur Lateinischen Formen-
lehre. Donaldson's *Varronianus*, ch. 6.

§ 4.

First Customary Rules mainly Religious.

It may be urged with justice that our picture of the
earliest Roman law must be entirely colored by the
source from which our materials are derived—that is, in
all probability, the books of the pontiffs. These officers,
it may be said, would naturally only record what enactments affected their own province, and the preponderance
of the quasi-religious element is therefore no proof that
legislation on that subject came first. In reply, the following points are to be considered. First, the priority of
rules of conduct (one can scarcely call them *laws*) upon
religious matters is in analogy with all that we know of

the early history of other nations. Second, the college
of Pontiffs, having undoubtedly at a later period custody
of the forms of secular law[a], is not likely, at an earlier,
to have excluded this important subject from its books.
Third, some of the most important and lasting principles
of the Roman law of persons can be distinctly traced to
a religious origin, and were, to the last, under the guardianship of religious officers.

Sacred law being, in the present point of view, only
considered as furnishing the source of secular law, matters
of mere ceremony and religious usage may be passed over
very briefly. The Litanies, for instance, of the Arval
and Salian religious guilds, interesting as they are from
being probably the oldest extant specimens of Latin, do
not here concern us. The imperatives addressed to human
beings which occur in these Litanies are merely rubrical
directions to the officiating brethren[b]. The 'law of the
spolia opima,' perhaps attributed to Numa and most probably taken from the pontifical books, merely states the
sacrifices to be made and the scale of reward to be given
on occasions so rare that but three are recorded[c]. More,
no doubt, of that generality of scope which characterizes
a law, is found in the following fragments, also coming to
us under Numa's name. 'Let no one quench a funeral-
pyre with wine'[d]. 'Let not a *pellex* touch an altar of
Juno: if such a one shall touch such an altar, let her,
with loosened hair, sacrifice to Juno a she-lamb'[e]. 'If
the lightning of Jove has killed a man let no one raise
him above the knees (*i.e.* of those around?).' Of which
the following is perhaps an explanation—'if a man has
been killed by lightning no funeral rites ought to be
performed for him'[f].

These and the like, extracted doubtless from the pontifical books, are rather maxims than laws. They are

mere statements of the religious feeling and sentiment current upon the matters to which they refer, and have scarcely a more authoritative aspect than those curious prohibitions which occur in the latter part of Hesiod's *Works and Days*ᵉ. Express sanction there is none: a practical one probably operated partly in fear of divine displeasure, partly in reluctance to incur the disapproval and lose the religious fellowship of the society in which one lives. It seems, however, not unlikely that some of the prohibitions, originally dictated by a purely religious feeling, came in later times to do duty, by formal enactment, some as sumptuary, some as sanitary laws, some as minor regulations for public order and decency. This certainly appears to be the case with much of the burial law of the Twelve Tables, which may be noticed here, as having but little bearing on the ordinary province of law, and as being also, perhaps, the mere regulation and reduction within due limits, of customs far older than the time of that legislation. 'Let no one bury or burn a dead man in the city'ʰ. 'Let no one make more' (ado, or perhaps, *sacrifice*, if *facere* be taken in its technical sense) 'than this' (doubtless some ceremonial previously specified): 'let no one smooth a funeral-pile with the adze'. 'After cutting down,' says Cicero, 'all pomp to three mourning-hoods and one stripe of purple and ten flute-players, the law does away also with *lamentation*' (formal manifestation of female sorrow). 'Let not women tear their cheeks nor make wailing for a funeral'.' In another passage from the same author, 'Let no one gather a dead man's bones wherewith in after-time to make a funeral'. In one from Pliny, an exception which has alone been preserved shews us the rule—a sumptuary law, forbidding decoration of the corpse. 'Whoso winneth a crown, he or his chattel (*i.e.* a slave or horse), for merit, if such

crown shall have been put on him or his father, let that
be without prejudice[m].' Closely connected with the last
passage is the following very curious testimony to the
advanced civilization of the Decemviral epoch. There is,
by the way, some consolation in finding that the de-
generacy of the modern, or (what is the same thing) the
superiority of the ancient, in the article of teeth, may not
be so certain as is often supposed. 'Neither let any one
put gold on (a corpse). Whoso shall have his teeth joined
with gold and one shall bury or burn him with it, let that
be without prejudice[n].' Last come two prohibitions, of
which Cicero has preserved us the matter but not the
exact words, one forbidding the erection of a new pile or
sepulchre within sixty feet of another's house, unless by
the owner's consent ; the other excepting the entrance to
a sepulchre or the sepulchre itself from usucapion[o].

Most of these directions and prohibitions refer to
matters in which the laity could take some part : a much
more extensive range was doubtless reserved by the religious colleges to themselves, and regulated by their own
bye-laws. The management of the Calendar, for instance,
we know to have been long kept in the hands of the
pontiffs, whose sole knowledge of court-days and days
proper for public business was a considerable source of
political power if not of emolument. The ancient treatment of this particular subject is shewn, not merely by
traditional institutions of Numa or Romulus[p], but by
the formula of the Pontifex minor which Varro has preserved. 'For five days I call on thee,' or 'for seven days
I call on thee' (as the Nones were on the fifth or seventh
day), 'Iuno Couella[q].' These words were said, on the
new moon being descried, by the Pontifex minor to the
people 'called' for the purpose to the 'Court of Calling.'
So that the first day of the month is said to have received

its name from this 'calling' of the Nones which settled its main subdivisions and its duration : there being thence eight days to the Ides and sixteen after[f]. The identification is certain of ' Iuno Couella' with the 'hollow moon' (κοίλη σελήνη), halfway between new and full. The time must have been early in which the great Roman goddess Juno was recognized, not by the speculations of philosophers but by the simple expressions of national religion, as an elemental deity. Without this clue, however, it would not be so easy to connect the name of ' the shining one' (Lucina)[g] with her province—the period namely of gestation, reckoned in those divisions of time which are marked by the planet.

a. Pomponius, Digest. 1. 2. 2. 6. Livy, 9. 46.

b. See for the Arvalian Litany Donaldson Varronianus ch. 6. § 2, for the fragments of the Salian hymns, ib. § 4. I do not bind myself to the interpretations there given.

c. Festus. *Opima spolia.*
.... M. Varro ait...testimonio esse libros pontificum in quibus sit pro primis spoliis boue pro secundis solitaurilibus pro tertiis agno publice fieri debere; esse etiam Pompili regis (emendation for *compelli reges*) legem opimorum spoliorum talem, &c.

d. Pliny, H. N. 14. 12.
Vino rogum ne respergito. See Festus *Resparsum uinum*, which, according to Ursinus' probable emendations of the Farnese fragment, means uinum rogo inspersum. A greater extravagance seems to have followed, in the *murrata potio*, the pouring of which over the dead was subsequently forbidden by the Twelve Tables as Festus (s.v.) tells us, quoting Varro's Antiquities. See below (note o) for Cicero's *sumptuosa respersio.*

e. Festus *Pellices* .... antiqui proprie eam pellicem nominabant quae uxorem habenti nubebat. cui generi mulierum etiam poena constituta est a Numa Pompilio hac lege, *pelles aram Iunonis ne tangito, si tanget...Iunoni crinibus demissis agnam feminam caedito.* I know no English word exactly rendering the old meaning of *pelles* according to Flaccus, 'quae uxorem habenti nubebat.' (See too Digest. 50. 16. 144.) Though (like *latro* and *scurra*) clearly holding a better position in early than in late times, a *pellex* would naturally, in either, be obnoxious to the *matrona* Iuno.

Zumpt (Anmerkk. p. 408) casts some doubt on the quotation under *pellices*, in which he recognizes the developed Latinity of a later period. It is quite possible, however, that the phrase to which I imagine his objection applies (*crinibus demissis*) may have been an interpolation, and the rest genuine.

f. Festus. *Occisum...*in Numae Pompili regis legibus scriptum esse, *si hominem fulmen Iouis* (Scaliger for *fulminibus*) *occisit ne supra genua tollito.* Et alibi, *homo si fulmine occisus est ei iusta nulla fieri oportet.*

Gifanius changes the words *et alibi* to *id est.* The latter passage is evidently of later date than the former. See Pliny H. N. 2. 54, 55, and generally the word *bidental* in lexicons and indices.

g. Opera et Dies. 695—762.

h. Cicero de Legibus 2. 23 § 58. *Hominem mortuom*, inquit lex in XII, *in urbe ne sepelito neue urito.*

i. Cicero de Legibus 2. 23. § 59.

Iam cetera in XII minuendi sumptus sunt lamentationisque funebris translata de Solonis fere legibus. *hoc plus*, inquit, *ne facito : rogum ascia ne polito :* nostis quae secuntur: discebamus enim pueri XII ut carmen necessarium, quas iam nemo discit. extenuato igitur sumptu tribus riciniis† et uincla† purpurae et decem tibicinibus tollit etiam lamentationem: *mulieres genas ne radunto neue lessum funeris ergo habento.*

The ablative tribus riciniis, &c., must be instrumental and mean '*by* (leaving) only three, &c.' I do not see the necessity for Schöll's interpolation *relictis*. For the untranslateable *et uincla* Orelli proposes *et uinclis;* Rubenius (de re uestiaria), *cum clauis;* Schöll, very ingeniously, *et uno clauo.* Compare Festus ' *Recinium* omne uestimentum quadratum ii qui XII interpretati sunt esse dixerunt †uir toga mulieres utebantur praetextum† clauo purpureo.' The corrupt passage is admirably emended by Lipsius, uer. (i.e. Verrius) togam *qua*, and Ursinus, praetextam.

Varro (de Lingua Latina 5. 132) derives the same word thus:— quod eo utebantur duplici ab eo quod dimidiam partem retrorsum iaciebant ab reiciendo *ricinium* dictum. It was palliolum *breue* according to Nonius. Corssen makes it *ausgedehnte.* Petit (Leges Atticae, clib. 6. tit. 8) takes these *ricinia* and the ἱμάτια mentioned in Plutarch's Solon (see next note) to have been for the *corpse*, but this view scarcely suits the Latin context, and Plutarch as probably means three flounces to the dress of each female mourner.

k. See the quotation in note *i.* Among the interpretations given in his time of the obsolete *lessum* Cicero prefers that of L. Aelius: 'lugubrem eiulationem:...quod eo magis iudico uerum esse quia lex Solonis id ipsum uetat.' His authority appears in § 64. postea quam ut scribit *Phalereus*, sumptuosa fieri funera et lamentabilia coepissent, Solonis lege sublata sunt: quam legem eisdem prope uerbis nostri decem uiri in decimam tabulam coniecerunt; nam de tribus riciniis et pleraque illa Solonis sunt. de lamentis uero expressa uerbis sunt *mulieres*, &c. A better authority for the meaning of *lessum* is Plautus' line (Truc. 4. 2. 22), Thetis quoque etiam lamentando lessum fecit filio. *Fecit* helps us to the meaning of *habere* in the law, where it is doubtless used as in the expressions habere iter, dialogum, &c.

To revert, however, to this alleged law of Solon, which is interesting as forming almost the only link between what we know of Athenian legislature and that of the Twelve Tables:—Demetrius Phalereus left Athens, in the same year in which Appius Claudius Caecus was consul, for Egypt. It was possibly during his comparative leisure in the latter country that his works were written, amongst others five books περὶ τῆς Ἀθήνησι νομοθεσίας (Diogenes Laertius 5. 5). He was himself, we are told by Cicero, the enactor of a sumptuary law on funerals: 'sumptum minuit non solum poena sed etiam tempore, ante lucem enim iussit efferri.' His treatise would no doubt contain recent as well as ancient legislation on the subject: nor is it to be supposed that he was more free than others from the invariable tendency to attribute as much as possible of extant law to some time-honored legislator. How much of what is commonly attributed to him can be connected, on historical grounds, with our own Alfred?

Demetrius' work has not come down to us, but it must have been in Cicero's hands, and it is clear that some sumptuary law therein contained must have coincided, in matters of minute detail, with the burial law of the Twelve Tables. The statement of Plutarch on the subject of Solon's law is as follows:—ἐπέστησε δὲ καὶ (ὁ Σόλων) ταῖς ἐξόδοις τῶν γυναικῶν καὶ ταῖς πένθεσι καὶ ταῖς ἑορταῖς νόμον ἀπείργοντα τὸ ἄτακτον καὶ ἀκόλαστον· ἐξιέναι μὲν ἱματίων τριῶν μὴ πλέον ἔχουσαν κελεύσας μηδὲ βρωτὸν ἢ ποτὸν πλείονος ἢ ὀβολοῦ φερομένην μηδὲ κάνητα πηχυαίου μείζονα μηδὲ νύκτωρ πορεύεσθαι πλὴν ἁμάξῃ κομιζομένην λύχνου προφαίνοντος. ἀμυχὰς δὲ κοπτομένων καὶ τὸ θρηνεῖν πεποιημένα καὶ τὸ κωκύειν ἄλλον ἐν ταφαῖς ἑτέρων ἀφεῖλεν. ἐναγίζειν δὲ βοῦν οὐκ εἴασεν οὐδὲ συντιθέναι πλέον ἱματίων τριῶν οἶδ' ἐπ' ἀλλότρια μνήματα βαδίζειν χωρὶς ἐκκομιδῆς.

The great historian whose loss we are now deploring (Mr Grote) takes the whole of this passage to refer to funerals (History of Greece, pt. 2. ch. 11). I do not think it certain that the first clause (ἐξιέναι μὲν…προφαίνοντος) may not belong rather to the subject of festivals. As to the latter clause (ἀμυχὰς δὲ…ἐκκομιδῆς) there is no doubt. Plutarch's lawgiver forbids, at funerals, disfigurement of the face, singing of composed dirges, wailing for a stranger (? hired lamentation), expensive sacrifices, extravagance in dress, and going to others' sepulchres, except for the actual carrying out of the corpse.

Very little of this appears in the law quoted by Demosthenes as Solon's (in Macart. 1071), ἐκφέρειν τὸν ἀποθανόντα τῇ ὑστεραίᾳ ᾗ ἂν προθῶνται πρὶν ἥλιον ἐξέχειν. βαδίζειν δὲ τοὺς ἄνδρας πρόσθεν ὅταν ἐκφέρωνται τὰς δὲ γυναῖκας ὄπισθεν. γυναῖκα δὲ μὴ ἐξεῖναι εἰσιέναι εἰς τὰ τοῦ ἀποθανόντος· μηδ' ἀκολουθεῖν ἀποθανόντι ὅταν εἰς τὰ σήματα ἄγηται ἐντὸς ἑξήκοντ' ἐτῶν γεγονυῖαν πλὴν ὅσαι ἐντὸς ἀνεψιαδῶν εἰσί· μηδ' εἰς τὰ τοῦ ἀποθανόντος εἰσιέναι ἐπειδὰν ἐξενεχθῇ ὁ νέκυς γυναῖκα μηδεμίαν πλὴν ὅσαι ἐντὸς ἀνεψιαδῶν εἰσίν.

This law, contained in a speech which was most likely composed before 354 B.C., therefore 36 years before the legislation of Demetrius could have commenced, includes a regulation (πρὶν ἥλιον ἐξέχειν) attributed by Cicero to him.

On the other hand it does *not* include the particulars in which the coincidence of the Solonian law, as reported by Cicero (from Demetrius), with that of the Twelve Tables is so remarkable. Upon the whole, I am inclined to believe, bold as the supposition may seem, that the particulars came from Roman to Greek rather than from Greek to Roman legislation. The comparative probability of the former nation borrowing from the latter or the latter from the former I must leave a matter of opinion ; merely remarking that any supposed improbability of interchange of ideas on law-making at all at this early period makes as much against the common theory as against that here advanced. If, then, Demetrius introduced in his legislation, or in his treatise, some of the Roman law, part of this may *possibly* have been attributed *by him* to Solon, and very probably by his readers Plutarch (Solon c. 23, p. 91) and Cicero, of whom the latter did, as we have seen, wrongly attribute a prior regulation to Demetrius. Should this view be correct, the otherwise remarkable coincidence in detail (e.g. between the tria ricinia and the τρία ἱμάτια) is no proof of a Greek origin for the Twelve Tables.

1. Cicero de Legibus 2. 24. § 60. Cetera item funebria quibus luctus augetur XII sustulerunt. *homini*, inquit, *mortuo ne ossa legito quo post funus faciat.* excipit bellicam peregrinamque mortem. This

prohibition seems to be directed against the practice of 'taking out of the ground' (excipere) remains supposed not to have been buried with due solemnity, in order to hold a solemn funeral afterwards. In this case a mere covering with earth (in proper form) sufficed to purify the family, which was, until such covering, *funesta*. *Funus*, strictly, is either incense-offering for the dead (Corssen Beit. 179), or burning of the corpse. See Servius on Aen. 2. 539: 3. 62. His notes on the whole account of Polydorus' burial are very interesting. An exception might naturally be made of those who had been laid in foreign earth or 'shovelled up into a bloody trench.' On the 'covering with earth' see Cicero de legibus 2. 22 § 55 and Varro de lingua Latina 5. 23. Si os exceptum est mortui ad familiam purgandam, donec in purgando humo est opertus (ut pontifices dicunt quoad inhumatus sit) familia funesta manet.

Schöll takes the passage quoted by Cicero to be against the *multiplication* of funeral rites, reading, with Schömann, after *faciat*, the words (which in the MSS. of the de legibus come a little lower) credo quod erat factitatum ut uni plura fierent lectique plures sternerentur: id quod ne fieret lege sanctum est. In favour of this view is perhaps Digest. 11. 8. 44. Vnius sepultura plura sepulcra efficere non potest.

m. Pliny H. N. 24. 5, 7. Ad certamina in circum per ludos et ipsi descendebant et servos suos equosque mittebant, inde illa XII tabularum lex, *qui coronam parit ipse pecuniaue eius uirtutis ergo duitur et* quam servi equine meruissent *pecunia partam* lege dici nemo dubitauit, quis ergo honos? ut ipsi mortuo parentibusque eius dum intus positus esset forisue ferretur sine fraude esset imposita. Pliny here gives the most probable interpretation of the curious expression *pecuniaue* eius. Of course this rendering is fatal to the alternative being between *pecunia* and *uirtus*. The reading *uirtutisue* must therefore be explained by inserting with Schöll *honoris* (see Festus under *Ergo* 'honoris uirtutisue ergo'), or, which seems simpler, by supposing the *ue* to have been the addition of some copier who imagined pecunia and uirtus to be here connected. The latter word, of course, means personal merit or conduct, as distinguished from luck: a very common use in Plautus. The following difficult word duitur may perhaps, on the strength of the MS. reading *arguitur*, be altered to *arduitur*, though some instance of what seems an unnecessary dissimilation should be found, before the occurrence of *ar* for *ad* before *d* can be considered satisfactory. Fortunately the preposition is not essential to the sense of the passage. *duitur* in point of verbal stem agrees

with *creduas, perduint,* &c. As to its temporal and modal part
Schöll justly objects to the emendation duitor, partly because the
MSS. afford no foundation for this reading, partly because the
imperative passive is not used in the simple style of the Twelve
Tables. We are then driven to a conditional sentence, the inser-
tion of *si* and the addition of words which certainly seem required
both by the above-quoted passage of Pliny and the parallel one of
Cicero. [*Si*] *arduitur* (or *duitur*) *ei* [*parentive eius se fraude esto.*]
Compare Cicero de Legibus 2. 24. § 60. Illa iam significatio
est laudis ornamenta ad mortuos pertinere quod coronam uirtute
partam et ei qui peperisset et eius parenti sine fraude esse lex im-
positam iubet. The *arduitur* or *duitur* of the protasis Schöll
takes to be a perfect future passive, comparing the rare forms fax-
itur, iussitur, turbassitur and mercassitur, and plŭi, lŭi, &c. from
plŭo, lŭo. See his very learned disquisition Legis XII Tabb. Reliqq. pp. 80—89. Corssen makes it present indicative. Ausspr.
2². p. 402.

n. Cicero de Legibus 2. 24. § 60. Qua in lege cum esset, *neue aurum
addito,* quam humane excipit (Orelli for *excipiat*) altera lex:
*cui auro dentes iuncti esunt, ast im cum illo sepeliet uretue, se
fraude esto.*

Schöll's emendation of the MS. *sepelleturetue* appears certain.
For the MS. *essent* I prefer Klotz' *esunt* (erunt) to his 'inchoative
with future signification' *escunt.* See however Schöll's note, pp.
98—100.

o. See Cicero de Legibus 2. 24 § 61. also Pomponius in Dig. 11. 8. 3.
I may here remark that I have omitted to notice other points of
extravagance, mentioned by Cicero as forbidden, but for which he
does not, as in the instances above cited, appear to quote the
words of the Twelve Tables. De Legibus 2. 24. 60. Haec praeterea
sunt in legibus: seruilis unctura tollitur (not tollitor, an attempt
of Manutius to turn this into a verbatim quotation) omnisque
circum potatio; quae et recte tolluntur neque tollerentur nisi
fuissent. nec sumptuosa respersio nec longae coronae nec acerrae
praetereuntur. (Bake for ne...ne...nec...praetereantur.)

p. Livy 1. 19. 20. Plutarch Numa 18—20. Macrobius Saturnalia 1.
12. 13.

q. Varro de L. L. 6. 27. Primi dies mensium nominati Calendae ab
eo quod his diebus calantur eius mensis Nonae a pontificibus
quintanae an septimanae sint futurae, in Capitolio in Curia Calabra sic: *dies te quinque calo, Iuno couella. septem dies te calo,
Iuno couella.*

r. See last note; also Macrobius Satt. 1. 15. 7.

5. Varro (de L. L. 5. 69) tells us that the Moon is called Iuno Lucina by the Latins. Etymologically the stem Iunon- points to Iou- (Ioui-) non-, and therefore cannot be called exactly a sister form of Ianus, though the two deities are certainly regarded as bearing a very close relationship to one another by Roman writers. See a quotation from Varro preserved in the Saturnalia 1. 9. 16. In sacris...inuocamus Ianum...Iununium, quasi non solum mensis Iannari sed mensium omnium ingressus tenentem: in ditione autem Iunonis sunt omnes Kalendae, unde et Varro libro quinto rerum diuinarum scribit Iano duodecim aras pro totidem mensibus dedicatas. The moon is *Iana* in Varro's Res Rust. 1. 37. 3. And Nigidius Figulus (Macrob. Satt. 1. 9. 8.) makes Iana and Ianus respectively moon and sun. The ancient and highly honored worship of the latter deity in Italy is well known. He is the 'god of gods' in the Salian hymns. Macrob. Satt. 1. 14 Saliorum quoque antiquissimis carminibus *deorum deus* canitur. He belongs too to an element-worship as 'lord of day in whom is the rising and the setting' (Servius on Aen. 7. 607), whence doubtless come all his associations with opening and shutting. By his creative and vivifying power he becomes an all-connecting all-embracing principle of Nature herself, binding the discordant elements toge-ther. So sings the augur Messalla, on this cherished national sub-ject almost a poet. Marcus etiam Messalla, Gn. Domiti in con-sulatu collega, idemque per annos LV augur, de Iano ita incipit: 'qui cuncta fingit eademque regit, aquae terraeque uim ac natu-ram grauem, ignis atque animae leuem...copulauit circumdato caelo.' Varro de lingua Latina 7. 27.

§ 5.

GENTES. SACRA. PATERFAMILIAS. CONFARREATIO. ARROGATIO.

THE ceremonial itself of the first Romans has perhaps little more than antiquarian interest: but the feeling with which that ceremonial was regarded, and the means employed for its maintenance, have exercised the most important influence on Roman legal institutions.

Some of the oldest religious guilds were clearly connected with particular localities; there were, for instance, the Salii Collini and the Salii Quirinales, both mentioned in the ancient Salian hymns[a]. Equally clear is it that certain rites were connected with particular *gentes:* the worship of Hercules with the Pinarian, originally associated, apparently on inferior terms, with a Potitian *gens* extinct at or at least after the time of Appius Claudius Caecus[b]; the ancient shepherd's festival of the Lupercalia with the Quinctian or Quinctilian *gens* of the Palatine and the Fabian *gens* of the Quirinal. The peculiar worship of Minerva was preserved, according to Servius and Varro, by the Nautii; that of the Sun is said by Flaccus to have originally appertained to the Aurelii[c]. In these cases it is, of course, possible that public or general *sacra* may have been committed to the charge of a particular *gens*, which is expressly stated of the Aurelii (see end of note *a*): but the probability seems at least as great that the public *sacra* were, at any rate in part, a developement or collection of the gentile. The institution of gentes, which we find at full growth in the earliest historical times, is a singular result of the Roman principle of family. We find a number of families (in the modern sense of the word) not merely bearing the same name but united by the tradition of a common ancestor, acting together in politics, going forth bodily on a colonizing expedition, involved in one common sentence of exile; above all, connected by peculiar and distinctive religious ceremonies, which the universal commonwealth, so far from discouraging, makes it an especial object to perpetuate. The impossibility, even in the earliest periods, of tracing any actual relationship between all the members of a *gens* seems to me shewn by the ancestors whom tradition has reported to us. The Aemilii come from Mamercus the

son of Pythagoras or Aemilius the grandson of Aeneas ; the
Antonii and Fabii from a son of Hercules ; the Caecilii
from a son of Vulcan ; the Calpurnii from a son of Numa ;
Iulus, Fusus, and Volesus are the very obvious ancestors
of the Iulii Furii and Valerii. It is scarcely possible that
the fiction cannot have been patent to any Roman who
ever devoted a thought to the subject. But it was a
fiction destined to exercise a more powerful influence than
many truths.

The real derivations of the *nomina* (gentile names) are
very doubtful. In some cases, perhaps, the small associations
which were to form the elements of a future community
may have derived their name, as did, according to Thucydides, the Hellenes, from a powerful chieftain round whom
they congregated ; in some, from their locality ; in some,
from a special pursuit or article of production⁴. Among
many other circumstances which point to unity of residence
as an essential characteristic of the earliest *gentes* is that
among the names of the Curiae, or wards, containing it is
said ten *gentes* each, some are clearly local while others
are as clearly gentile⁵. Nor can one see a better reason
for the gentile names of many of the rustic tribes, than
that the lands of the *gens* lay mainly together and in that
particular district. But whatever the circumstances were
which brought it together or gave it a name, it is clear
that the original *gens* was not considered to have sufficient coherence unless united by the fact of a common
worship and what must in most cases have been the
fiction of a common descent. With later incomers the
same feeling might not exist, or, if it did exist and did
lead to the similar formation of newer societies, these
would naturally be kept to a certain extent on a lower
footing by the older, which must soon have assumed that
aristocratic character whereby, in historical times, we

know them so well. This is at least a possible way of
accounting for the existence of Greater and Lesser (or
perhaps Older and Younger) patrician, and some few
plebeian, *gentes*. These distinctions perhaps indicate two
successive barriers drawn round a privileged class. The
first, however, disappeared at a time of which we have no
authentic record, while the breaking down of the second
forms one of the most interesting chapters of history.
From the influx of persons having no *gens*[f], perhaps from
the emigration, too, of original members, the locality of
gentes would naturally become less definite, and the *sacra*
—bond and sign of the immemorial aristocratic relationship—more prized. So we find their maintenance watched
over by the gentile assembly of the Curiae, or their
religious officers, with the most jealous care. The obligation to their periodic performance must have been considered as resting upon each *familia* (or body of persons
who really could trace their descent from some actual
common ancestor); upon each head of a household who
had no lineal ascendant living; possibly even upon each
male member[g].

It may perhaps have been partly from his responsible
position as joint depositary of the *sacra*, that the Head
of the Family (*paterfamilias*) came to exercise the asto-
nishingly despotic power known as the *patria potestas*.
This relation, though founded upon patriarchal principles
common to all infant nations, reached at Rome such un-
usual developement that it seems to have borrowed both
in spirit and terminology from the idea of capture in war.
This was, indeed, in all probability, with the warlike
Nation of Spearmen (*bellicosi Quirites*) the fundamental
idea of property generally. As the spear was a symbol,
so was the strong-hand a name of their rough legal ownership: and this expressive designation of forcible posses-

sion, which remained technical in the case of the wife, was doubtless originally applied to the whole of the family as well[h]. At any rate the power of a *paterfamilias*, whencesoever derived, appears at first to have differed but little from that of an owner over chattels, and more-over to have been generally indestructible except by death[i]. Its determination by three sales was probably a later innovation sanctioned by the Twelve Tables: the still later dispensing with two of the sales in the case of descendants other than sons was effected by a strict in-terpretation of the word *filium* in the clause referred to, a general extinguishment of paternal power by sale being assumed, which was certainly not law in the oldest times[j].

His extreme rights, however, can scarcely have been exercised by the father who had allowed the son to con-tract legal marriage with a free woman, though for a formal enactment on the subject we have mere tradition[k]. Again, it was obviously necessary, to avoid the clashing of two authorities, that a daughter who passed into the marital passed out of the paternal power.

Marriage was doubtless, in the oldest times, looked upon mainly as the means of producing those descendants of pure blood who should perpetuate the *sacra*. Accord-ing to the principles of the close aristocracy that we are now considering, principles which lie deep in the founda-tion of Roman law, it is probable that no union was re-garded as a proper marriage unless each party belonged to some *gens*. Practice would, of course, tend to break down this hard rule, but it was certainly the subject of an enactment in the Twelve Tables subsequently repealed by the rogation or plebiscitum of Canuleius[l]. Such an enactment can have been no new idea, but rather an attempt to erect into *law* a *customary* barrier which was crumbling away. It is interesting to remark that it is the interference with public and private *ceremonial rites* likely to result from unions between a patrician and a plebeian which was, according to Livy, alleged as a reason for this prohibition[m].

We are therefore prepared to expect that connection with the *sacra* which we find in the oldest form of marriage. A genuine custom is no doubt here preserved to us by Dionysius under the pretended form of a law of Romulus—'that a woman uniting herself in marriage with a man according to the sacred laws becomes a sharer in everything, property and *sacra*[n].' This 'sacred marriage' he explains to be the Roman *confarreation*. It was an emblematical partaking together by the bride and groom of the simplest form of food, perhaps a wheaten cake, under the officiation of the Pontifex Maximus and Flamen Dialis[o]. The use of certain solemn words was necessary in this ceremony, as also the presence of ten witnesses, who are, with great probability, believed by Mommsen to represent the ten wards (*Curiae*) of the oldest Roman constitution[p]. Similarly the thirty lictors of far later times appeared for the thirty Curies[q], and the five witnesses to mancipation, in all probability, for the five classes[r].

In connection both with the *sacra* and the subject of marriage, viewed with reference to its original object (*liberum procreandorum caussa*), there remains to be noticed the important principle of representation of a deceased person. It was obviously desirable, to prevent the memory of the *sacra* perishing by the death of the *pater-familias*[s], that he should leave behind him some one to fill his place and perform his duties. With the duties were naturally associated the means of the deceased; and there is little doubt that the succession was originally regarded as matter of public concern, to be settled by

recognized customary rules and not by the wish of any
individual. In the language of later writers, the first
heredes were *legitimi* rather than **testamentarii**. We are
dealing, in fact, with a period when there was no *testament* at all. Those who having been in the power of the
paterfamilias, became, on his death, *sui iuris*—under their
own control —were also the *sui heredes*, ' takers by their own
right' of *his* rights, his obligations, and his means. These
successors, if minors or females, were protected, and at
the same time prevented from squandering the family
inheritance, by a 'surveillance' (*tutela*) of those next entitled, older in all probability than the law of the Twelve
Tables in which it was recognized and regulated. Whether
there was ever one principal 'taker' or 'master' we cannot
say: no distinct traces of primogeniture appear in our
authorities[1].

It was where there was likely to be a failure in the
succession, an extinction of a family and consequent di-
minution of the means or agents for perpetuating the
sacra, that the wishes of the childless master of a household were first recognized. By a vote of the gentile
comitia curiata he could, subject to the sanction of the
pontiffs, *arrogate*, or take to himself by question put[a], any
youth having attained puberty and not subject to the
patria potestas, to be his own son. Enquiry was made as
to the age of the arrogator and the non-probability of his
having issue of his own body: also as to the fortune of
the person taken in arrogation, which would, it must be
remembered, become the property of his new father. No
objection having been raised by the assembly—including,
of course, those interested in the natural succession to the
arrogate —or by the presiding pontiffs, it was put and
carried in the form of a regular bill that e.g. ' L. Valerius
should be in law as completely the son of L. Titius as if

born of L. Titius as father (and his wife as) mother of a family, and that Titius should have over Valerius power of life and death as a father has in the case of his son[w].'
The perfect substitution, in a Roman mind, of the legal relation arising from arrogation or adoption, for the natural one, which gives rise to many expressions familiar enough to the reader of Tacitus but sounding strangely to modern ears, is here expressed in plain words[x].

This subject of arrogation is very interesting, on the one hand as being so clearly connected with the *gentile* system, and especially (since under the pontifical sanction) with the preservation of the *sacra*; on the other, as perhaps leading the way to the earliest allowed will-making. For the testament made in the *comitia calata* tallies so closely in point of the assembly where its first and commonest execution took place (see below § 23), as well as of the presiding authorities, with *arrogation*, that one cannot but regard it as a result or development of that ancient practice. It is, however, more convenient to treat the *testamentum calatis comitiis* in a subsequent section, together with the form of testation by which it was ultimately superseded (§ 23).

a. Servius on Aen. 8. 284.

b. Id. Aen. 8. 270. Festus *Potitium et Pinarium.* Macrobius Saturnn. 3. 6. 12—14.

c. Mommsen Hist. 1. 4. (p. 55 n. of tr.) Servius Aen. 5. 704 'Tum senior Nautes,' Festus *Fauiani,* [Quinctiliani Luperci], and *Aureliam.*

d. Thuc. 1. 3. Association round a powerful protector was certainly the original relation of *clientes* to their *patronus.* Nor is it impossible that such was the origin of those *gentes* whose names denote a personal peculiarity or quality, which may have characterized their founder. Instances are Albia, Opimia, Flauia, Fuluia, Heluia, Liuia, Nacuia, Catia, Canidia, Claudia, Licinia, Aquilia, Duilia, Silia, Turpilia. The numeral names too, ranging from *fifth* to *ninth* and perhaps *last* (Quinctia, Nonia, Postumia), **may** indicate the foundation of new families by *cadets* of enterprise. The Fabii, Cornificii, Fabricii, Porcii, Furnii, Falcidii, Ve rii. Hortensii must surely have been named from occupation or product (see Pliny H. N. 18. 3.). This view is quite consistent with a determinate locality, which each trade usually has in infant states. Names directly from locality are Pontius, Marius, perhaps Tigellius, and others of which we might have more satisfactory etymologies if we knew the topography of early Rome better. The **Fla**minii and Antistii must have been priestly families. The Aurelii were supposed, according to Flaccus, to have been named from the sun, because a place was publicly assigned to them by the Roman people in which to make sacrifice to the sun. It was from this, he says, that they were called *Auseli*. (Festus *Aureliam*) The word may be traced to the same root *-us* from which comes Aurora (Curtius Grundzüge 612, p. 371). This is an instance of a *plebeian* gens, perhaps later incomers, (familiam ex Sabinis oriundam Festus loc. cit.) traditionally connected with special *sacra* which had been made matter of public interest.

e. Mommsen Hist. 1. 5 (p. of tr. 73). It is true that the identity of the *decuriae* with *gentes* is anything but certain. This, however, does not affect the inference drawn from the names of the Curiae, which may be re-stated as follows:—Some names of Curiae are gentile, others local; it is probable that the same principle would be followed in naming all; therefore it is probable that at least those *gentes* had a definite locality. The word Curia itself means nothing but house (Corssen, Ausspr. 1.²353)—the house, doubtless, of meeting and worship common to each small original association (see Festus, *Curia*). Here, as elsewhere, it will be seen, that *agglutination* is considered as the more probable order of things than *subdivision*, in the infancy of a state. Besides the evidence of antiquity and inferences drawn from analogy, to this effect, it may fairly be asked what possible *object* could the traditional founder have in splitting up his little kingdom?

f. Livy 10. 8. Semper ista audita sunt eadem, penes uos auspicia esse uos solos *gentem habere*.

g. Heineccius Antiqq. L. 1. c. 1. App. 71. Livy 5. 46. Sacrificium erat statum in Quirinali colle genti Fabiae. ad id faciendum G. Fabius Dorso Gabino cinctu sacra manibus gerens . . . . in Quirinalem collem peruenit. The Dorsones cannot have been the leading family among the Fabii—compared, for instance, with the Vibulani. Nor is it likely that the individual (called by Camillus c. 52 *adolescens*) was even head of this particular family.

h. As the son *manu* mittebatur it is fair to conclude that he must at some time have been said to be in the *manus*, as well as the wife. On the subsidiary ceremonies of marriage indicative of capture (see Festus *Rapi*, and the 4th explanation of *Coelibari hasta*) I do not lay any special stress. They are paralleled by the oldest customs in this behalf amongst most nations.

The hasta was the well-known symbol of Quiritarian ownership in the old Centumviral Court, as was its representative in the *actio per sacramentum* (Gaius, Comm. 4. § 16). With regard to *Quirites* I very much prefer the view accepted by Mommsen (Hist. 1. 5 tr. pa. 78 n.) to any other, viz. that they were the individual warriors as distinguished from the collective *populus.* In this view populus Romanus [et] Quirites and the *crux* populus Romanus Quiritium are both quite intelligible; as is the pathetic funeral proclamation ' that warrior is given to the land where all things are forgotten ' (see Festus *Quirites*...ollus Quiris leto datus, and *Letum*). There seems no objection to the derivation from *Curis,* a spear, which need not involve belief in an intermediate town *Cures* or hero *Quirinus* (Festus *Curis,* Ovid Fasti 2. 477). I am glad to find Mr Seeley (Livy 1. p. 72) agreeing with the *spearman* derivation of *Quirites,* though the support which he apparently claims from Festus' *Pilumnoe poploe*...velut pilis uti assueti...is not unquestionable. See Curtius Grundzüge 260. Corssen (Ausspr. 2. 357) prefers the derivation from Cures.

i. Dionysius probably gives a true account of the old *patria potestas,* though he attributes its institution to Romulus. Antiqq. Rom. 2. 26. ἅπασαν ὡς εἰπεῖν ἔδωκεν ἐξουσίαν πατρὶ καθ' υἱοῦ καὶ παρὰ πάντα τὸν τοῦ βίου χρόνον ἐάν τε εἴργειν ἐάν τε μαστιγοῦν ἐάν τε δέσμιον ἐπὶ τῶν κατ' ἀγρὸν ἔργων κατέχειν ἐάν τε ἀποκτιννύναι προαιρῆται.

He makes the same authority place a restriction upon the *exposure* of sons and first daughters (2. 15). This practice, with regard to female infants, must have obtained, quite as a matter of course, to near the time of Terence (Hautontim. 4. 1. 13—24). Instances of nearly every kind of severity mentioned by Dionysius will be found in the biographies of the Manlii, who seem to have anticipated the 'Fairchild Family.' Civil death and the few other ways (besides emancipation) by which the *patria potestas* came to be terminated will be found in Gaius Comm. 1. 128—131. Iustin. Instt. 1. tit. 12. On the *patria potestas* see generally Mommsen's Hist. 1. 5. and Maine's Ancient Law, ch. 5.

j. Gaius Comm. 1. 132. filius quidem ter [mancipatus sui iuris fit, ceteri] uero liberi siue masculini sexus siue femiuini una manci-

patione exeunt de parentium potestate: lex enim xii tantum in
persona filii de tribus mancipationibus loquitur [his] uerbis: *si
pater filium ter uenum duuit filius* a patre liber esto. cf. Ulpian.
fr. 10. 1.

k. Dion. Antiqq. 2. 27. ἐν οἷς (sc. τοῖς τοῦ Νομᾶ νόμοις) . . . οὕτω γε-
γράπται ἐὰν πατὴρ υἱῷ συγχωρήσῃ γυναῖκα ἀγαγέσθαι κοινωνὸν ἐσομέ-
νην ἱερῶν τε καὶ χρημάτων κατὰ τοὺς νόμους μηκέτι τὴν ἐξουσίαν εἶναι
τῷ πατρὶ πωλεῖν τὸν υἱόν. For, says Plutarch, δεινὸν ἡγεῖτο τὴν ὡς
ἐλευθέρῳ γεγαμημένην γυναῖκα δούλῳ συνοικεῖν. Numa 17.

l. Livy 4: 4, 6. Dionys. Antiqq. 10. 60. Cicero de Rep. 2, 37. § 63.

m. Livy 4. 2. colluuionem gentium perturbationem auspiciorum publi-
corum priuatorumque afferre (Canuleium). 6. interroganti tribuno cur plebeium consulem fieri non oporteret, ut fortasse uere
sic parum utiliter in praesens certamen respondit (alter e consulibus) quod nemo plebeius auspicia haberet, ideoque Xuiros conubium diremisse, ne incerta prole auspicia turbarentur.

n. Dion. Antiqq. 2. 25. ἦν δὲ τοιόσδε ὁ νόμος γυναῖκα γαμετὴν κατὰ νόμους
ἱεροὺς συνελθοῦσαν ἀνδρὶ κοινωνὸν ἁπάντων εἶναι χρημάτων τε καὶ
ἱερῶν. ἐκάλουν δὲ τοὺς ἱεροὺς οἱ παλαιοὶ γάμους Ῥωμαϊκῇ προσηγορίᾳ
περιλαμβάνοντες Φαρράκια ἐπὶ τῆς κοινωνίας τοῦ φαρρὸς ὃ καλοῦμεν
ἡμεῖς ζέαν. cf. Pliny hist. nat. 18. 3. Tacit. Ann. 4. 16.

o. See last note, also Servius on Georg. 1. 31. tribus modis apud
ueteres nuptiae fiebant, usu..., farre cum per pontificem maximum
et dialem flaminem per fruges et molam salsam coniungebantur,
unde confarreatio appellabatur, ex quibus nuptiis patrimi et matrimi nascebantur, &c. The *praetextati pueri* who escorted a
bride to her new home were (or should be) patrimi et matrimi
whose parents were living. See Festus *Patrimi*.

p. Mommsen Hist. 1. 5. tr. p. 73. n.

q. Festus *Triginta lictores.*

r. See below, § 21.

s. Cicero de Legibus 2. 19. Hinc iura pontificum auctoritate conse-
cuta sunt ut ne morte patris familias sacrorum memoria occideret
iis essent ea adiuncta ad quos eiusdem morte pecunia ueniret.
Bake's reading, who, I think, satisfactorily defends this passage
against Madvig. The desire to secure persons *qui sacra facerent*
is made by Gaius (Comm. 2. 52, 55) the reason why possession
with knowledge of another's right was allowed to constitute usu-
capio of an inheritance.

t. Flaccus may connect *heres* ('apud antiquos pro domino ponebatur')
with *herus*; but nothing very certain as to the original idea of the
word can be inferred from Plautus Menaech. 3. 2. 12. Dr Donaldson's *her-ed-* from *haer-uad-* (Umbrian *here* 'take', Skr. hṛi, and

uad- 'bail') is perhaps fanciful as to the second part. Corssen does not offer an explanation of the d, which he merely compares with that of merce-d- and of the common suffix do. As to the first part of the word he agrees with Donaldson, considering *heres* to be Erb-*nehmer* (Ausspr. 1. 468) from the same root as *herus* (ib. 101), the old Latin *hir* (cf. Lucilius cited by Cicero, de Finibus 2. 8. § 23) and the Sanskrit *har* 'nehmen.'

As to the equal sharing of *heredes* see Gaius, Comm. 3. 1—8, Iust. Instt. 3. Tit. 1, and Dionysius 2. 25 where he speaks of the wife's right to succession as a daughter, making her take an equal share τοῖς παισίν, as if these also took equally.

u. Gaius, Comm. 1. 99. populi auctoritate adoptamus eos qui sui uiris sunt, quae species adoptionis dicitur arrogatio, quia et is qui adoptat rogatur id est interrogatur an uelit eum quem adoptaturus sit iustum sibi filium esse, et is qui adoptatur rogatur an id fieri patiatur, et populus rogatur an id fieri iubeat. The last is of course the true reason for the word.

w. Aulus Gellius Noctt. Att. 5. 19. Arrogantur hi qui cum sui iuris sunt in alienam seso potestatem tradunt eiusque rei ipsi auctores fiunt. sed arrogationes non temere nec inexplorate committuntur: nam comitia arbitris pontificibus praebentur quae curiata appellantur, aetasque eius qui arrogare uolt, an liberis potius gignundis idonea sit, bonaque eius qui arrogatur ne insidiose appetita sint consideratur . . adrogari non potest nisi iam uesticeps. (Festus s. v.) arrogatio autem dicta quia genus hoc in alienam familiam transitus per populi rogationem fit. eius rogationis uerba haec sunt: uelitis iubeatis uti L. Valerius L. Titio tam iure legeque filius siet quam si ex eo patre matreque familias eius natus esset utique ei uitae necisque in eum potestas siet uti patri endo filio est. haec ita uti dixi ita uos Quirites rogo.

No *woman* could be arrogated quoniam cum feminis nulla comitiorum communio est. ib.

x. e.g. of Augustus 'multa Antonio dum interfectores *patris* ulciscerctur . . concessisse.' The *pater* is the 'mightiest Julius.' Ann. 1. 9. Tiberius, too, asserts (se) de honoribus parentis consulturum (Ann. 1. 7), where the *parens* is Augustus.

y. Cicero pro Domo Sua 13. § 34 on Clodius' adoption, or, strictly speaking, arrogation. 'quae . . caussa cuique sit adoptionis, quae ratio generum ac dignitatis, quae sacrorum, quaeri a pontificum collegio solet . . . quid sacra Clodiae gentis cur intereunt, quod in te est? quae omnis notio pontificum, cum adoptarere, esse debuit.'

§ 6.

OFFENCES WITHIN THE FAMILY. FIRST SANCTIONS.

THE customary law which has been hitherto considered, whether remaining mere custom or formalized into the few quasi-statutory maxims which have come down to us, alike lacked that important element of law proper— an express sanction. There are, however, other 'laws' in which a sanction is expressed though not clearly defined. The reputed authors of these fragments, if of little value in fixing an exact date, may yet perhaps justify us in referring the latter generally to the regal period, when backed by the surer evidence of antiquity of form. **As** to the *relative* priority of these 'laws,' which must to a certain extent enter into our consideration of them, it is most difficult to avoid that besetting sin of all antiquarians, historical or philological, to make order of time and intrinsic antiquity alternately prove one another. Keeping the latter as much as possible distinct, we find that, in respect of *form*, there are in the fragments attributed to the Kings two instances of Indo-Germanic terminations all but unique in Latin and foreign to our remnants of the Twelve Tables[e]. Doubtless the latter, as being in practical use, may have been altered to at least a more modern spelling than that of their enactment: but the non-alteration of the former is in itself an evidence of their more venerable and therefore more antique character. The inflexibility of religious formularies or dicta is well known. Here, too, subject-matter affords us independent evidence of relative antiquity. The earliest historical views that we can get of the Roman people coincide with their most permanent usages and most

venerable constitutional forms in pointing to one conclusion—that *religion*, connected with or rather inclusive
of the idea of family relationship, was the first bond
between the small associations which united to form
Rome. It is in accordance with this general conclusion,
and moreover with what we know of the earliest history
of other nations also, that we shall be disposed to consider
those penal enactments the earliest, in which crimes and
offences are regarded as *sins*, and in which the penalty is
religious in form—though doubtless in effect it differed
widely from the *brutum fulmen* of a modern ecclesiastical
sentence. This view of priority will be confirmed if we
find that the offences themselves which are thus prohibited are those committed against the quasi-religious
parental authority which lies at the very root of the
oldest Roman institutions. The nascent criminal legislature, however, to which I refer, must be clearly distinguished from any purely patriarchal jurisdiction. At
the earliest period of which we have any knowledge, the
community was in existence as well as the family. Of
any *regular* parental judicature we must agree with
Mommsen that there is not a trace to be found[a]. Tradition has doubtless recorded several instances in which
the paternal power was exercised in accordance with what
would probably have been the sentence of a judge proper.
But such proceedings were clearly of an arbitrary character, depending entirely upon the irresponsible will and
pleasure of the offender's *owner*, i.e. the *paterfamilias*.
The latter is, of course, at once distinguished from a
judge by the fact that it was in his option whether he
should take any proceedings at all. Thus, to anticipate
for a moment the typical case of Horatius, we may admit
a prior quasi-jurisdiction over the case of sister-murder,
appertaining to the father[b]; but, as there is no security

to the public for its exercise, so, even when exercised, it
is no bar to a public trial. Whereas, in the fragments
about to be cited, it is evident that the parent (who may
of course even be a paterfamilias) is the complainant and
that the sentence is the sentence of the community,
whether a gens or an association of gentes.

Festus, in illustration of the word *plorare*, which
he says among the ancients evidently signified to com-
plain, quotes as follows:—In the laws of Romulus and
Tatius 'If a son's wife......let her be devoted to the
deities presiding over parents.' Among the laws of
Servius Tullius is this, 'If a son beat a parent and the
latter shall have complained, let the son be devoted to
the deities presiding over parents[c].' Then follows a further explanation of the word *plorassit*, which, though
mutilated, shews the *complaint* here mentioned to have
been considered by the writer as equivalent to a formal
indictment in later times.

In the first of the two quotations the offence of the
son's wife may be assumed similar in character to that of
the son, and Dr Donaldson supplies the lacuna accordingly[d]. Both prohibitions therefore are directed against
purely family offences, and both are furnished with the
same sanction, devotion to the gods of the family. What
this *sacratio* amounted to we have to learn from other
sources. Dionysius, who, as we have seen, makes the
patria potestas originate in an enactment of Romulus,
would appear to leave violations of filial duty for the
cognizance and punishment of the paterfamilias, supported or at least unopposed by popular feeling[e]. In
relations, however, between patron and client—a connection which had nothing to do with community of descent,
and which is also attributed by Dionysius, in substance
as well as in accidents, to Romulus — he represents

breaches of duty as checked by a mere public sanction.
If either patron or client were convicted of committing
any one of certain specified offences he was liable to
Romulus' law of treason. There is an interesting analogy
between this view of such offences and that taken by our
own common law in cases of murder when the murderer
owed a special private allegiance to the victim. Murder
by a servant of his master, by a wife of her husband, by
an ecclesiastical person of his superior, was *petit treason*
and visited with severer penalties than the ordinary
crime[f].

For the less serious offences, enumerated by Dionysius,
between patron and client 'the convicted person might be
killed by any that would, as a sacrifice to the infernal Dis.
For it was a custom with the Romans, when they willed
any to be killed with impunity, to dedicate their bodies
to some of the gods, especially to those of the infernal
regions[g].' A modern British practice, well known at least
to our charitable neighbours, was apparently visited by
Roman law with the same penalty as above mentioned.
Romulus enacted a law, says Plutarch, that the man who
sold his wife should be sacrificed to the infernal gods[h].

A great deal of Dionysius and a great deal more of
Plutarch comes doubtless from the love of moralising about
good old times which never existed; still we cannot refuse
to see some core of reality and some practical effect in the
sacratio when we find it used as an important political
expedient in undoubtedly historical transactions. Passing
over the law which Livy says was directed against attempts
to revive monarchy 'by devoting the life and goods' of the
culprit[i], we come to the *sacrosanct* tribunes of the first
secession[k], who, whatever the date of introduction or technical meaning of this term, were undoubtedly protected by
a sentence of *ipso facto* outlawry against any one who

violated their person or privileges. This sentence, Livy says, originally depended upon *religion*, but was made on the expulsion of the decemvirs a legal enactment[1]. A law passed with this particular sanction was a *lex sacrata*, of which Livy gives us other instances[m]. Cicero distinctly recognises this penalty in two passages[n].

The best authority, however, is that of Festus, who tells us that *sacratae leges* are those in which it is provided that whoever shall have done any thing against them be devoted (*sacer*) to some of the gods, with his family and property: and that a *homo sacer* is 'he whom the people hath sentenced for a crime; neither is it right for him to be *sacrificed*, but he who slayeth such a one is not found guilty of parricide (see below, § 7), for it is provided by the first tribunician law, that if any shall have slain him who is *sacer* by this plebiscite the slayer be no parricide[o].'

Mommsen takes the *sacratio* to have been, in the case of the tribunes, a real outlawry: whoever laid hands upon them was regarded not merely as forfeited to the vengeance of the gods, but also as outlawed and proscribed among men[p]. But as to the older sentence his opinion is different. 'Not that the person accused (*sacer*) was outlawed; such an outlawry, inconsistent in its very nature with all civil order, was only an exceptional occurrence in Rome—an aggravation of the religious curse at the time of the quarrels between the orders. It was not the province of the civil authorities, still less that of the individual burgess or of the wholly powerless priest, to carry into effect the divine curse; the life of the person accursed was forfeited not to man but to the gods[q].'

Zumpt, also, admitting that there may have been a time when the *sacratio capitis* was more than a mere sentence of excommunication, places that time at the safe distance of a 'pre-Roman period[1].' I cannot reconcile these views with the cumulus of evidence above-quoted; or help believing that the sentence *sacer esto* involved more than religious penalties even when it only existed—to borrow Livy's phrase—*religione*, not *lege*. That it was originally a religious sentence there is little doubt—proclaimed probably by the chief priests either solely or as presidents of a burgess-assembly, on complaint by the injured member of a family. The latter seems more probable, as answering to the 'sentence of the people' mentioned by Festus, on which the property of the *sacer* was considered as confiscated and his person placed out of the protection of the law. For the final words of the plebiscite are surely not so much the creation of a new as an affirmation of the old impunity for a slayer of the *sacer*, which impunity might possibly have been regarded as taken away by an intermediate statute against homicide in general.

It must be remembered, as against the objection of Mommsen, that this rough execution of justice dates from the very earliest times, when that developed civil order, with which it is no doubt inconsistent, had as yet no existence. Probably the sentence in practice only amounted to exile: but, even if taken in its harsher sense, the general right, in *all* persons belonging to a community, patriarchal or otherwise, of putting to death an outlaw, is not without parallel either in our own traditional common law, or in the reputed statute law of Athens, or in the oldest extant history of a capital crime[2].

a. Mommsen Hist. 1. 11. pp. 157—8 tr.

b. Zumpt Criminal-Recht des Röm. Republik. Absch. 1. c. 7. p. 91.

c. Plorare flere nunc significat et cum praepositione implorare id est inuocare. in regis Romuli et Tati legibus *si nurus…sacra diuis parentum estod.* in Serui Tulli haec est *si parentem puer uerberit ast olle plorassit puer diuis parentum sacer esto,* id est, inclamarit dix…[erit diem according to Müller's most probable restoration.]

In the first quotation the final *d* of the 3rd sing. imperative is a mark of antiquity almost unique in Latin, though instances are found in the Oscan *estud factud licitud* of the Bantine tablet. Compare the Vedic *tarpatât* (τερπέτω) Bopp, Vergl. Gram. § 470. The second quotation, it will be observed, wants the *d*, as do the imperatives of the Twelve Tables.

In the second quotation *uerberit*, which Müller apparently takes to be present subjunctive, is, I think, better regarded by Schöll (xii Tabb. Reliquiae, p. 83) as present indicative of the 3rd conjugation. *Ast* is of course equivalent to *autem* (Festus *ast.* Labbacus = ἐὰν δέ), see Plautus Capt. 3. 5. 25.

Si ego hic peribo ast illo ut dixit non redit
at erit mi hoc factum mortuo memorabile.   Schöll. p. 111.

d. Varronianus, c. 5. § 5. Dr Donaldson restores what may have been the old spelling, *sei nuros parentem [uerbesit ast ole plorasit] saera*, &c. It seems, in my present point of view, safer and better to give these fragments merely as they occur in good editions of the authors by whom they are quoted. Müller's remark is not a bad one, ‘oleum et operam mihi perdidisse uidentur qui regum legibus antiquitatis illam robiginem reddere studuerunt quam iam tum detersum esse apparet cum in Papirianum ius reciperentur.’

e. Antiqq. Rom. 2. 26 end.

f. Stephen's Blackstone 6. 4. Hale, 1 P. C. c. 29. See 25 Edw. 3rd, st. 5, c. 2.

g. Antiqq. Rom. 2. 10. This chapter contains an interesting account of the reciprocal rights and duties of patron and client. The relation bears an obvious parallel to that of lord and vassal. Stephen's Blackstone, 2. pt. 1. ch. 2. ‘of Tenures.’ In both cases, doubtless, the members of the privileged class gathered round them and attached to them the non-privileged as long as they could. When too numerous to be attached, the latter became a definite political order, with a grievance.

As to breaches of duty in this relation Dionysius says, εἰ δέ τις ἐξελεγχθείη τούτων τι διαπραττόμενος ἔνοχος ἦν τῷ νόμῳ τῆς προδοσίας ὃν ἐκύρωσεν ὁ Ῥωμύλος. τὸν δὲ ἁλόντα τῷ βουλομένῳ κτείνειν ὅσιον ἦν ὡς θῦμα τοῦ καταχθονίου Διός· ἔθος γὰρ Ῥωμαίοις ὅσους ἐβούλοντο νηποινὶ τεθνάναι τὰ τούτων σώματα θεῶν ὁτῳδήτινι μάλιστα δὲ τοῖς καταχθονίοις κατονομάζειν.

h. Plut. Romulus 32. τὸν δ᾽ ἀποδόμενον γυναῖκα (ἔθηκε νόμον) θύεσθαι χθονίοις θεοῖς.

i. Liv. 2. 8. See too 3. 55.

k. Liv. 2. 33.

l. Liv. 3. 55. Cum religione inuiolatos eos tum lege etiam fecerunt sauciendo ut qui tribunis plebis aedilibus iudicibus decemuiris nocuisset eius caput Ioui sacrum esset familia ad aedem Cereris Liberi Liberaeque uenum iret.   See too Dionys. Antiqq. 6. 89.

m. Liv. 3. 32: 7. 41: 9. 39: 36. 38.

n. Pro Balbo 14. 33.   Sanctiones sacrandae sunt aut genere ipso aut obtestatione legis aut poenae cum caput eius qui contra fecerit consecratur.   Frag. pro Tullio 5. 47. recitauit...legem antiquam de legibus sacratis quae iubeat impune occidi eum *qui tribunum pleb. pulsauerit.*

o. Festus *Sacratae leges* and *sacer mons.*   At homo sacer est is quem populus indicauit ob maleficium ; neque fas est eum immolari sed qui occidit parricidi non damnatur; nam lege tribunicia prima cauetur, *si quis eum qui eo plebei scito sacer sit occiderit, parricida ne sit.*

p. Mommsen's Hist. 2. 2. tr. p. 282.

q. ib. 1. 12 tr. p. 184.

r. Criminal-recht Absch. 1. p. 128.   Cf. 3. 5. p. 393.

s. See Blackstone 4. c. 24, on the other hand Hale P. C. 1. c. 42. The original source of Blackstone's statement I do not know.   It is *not* Coke on Lytt. § 128.   For Attic law, compare Demosthenes, 3rd Philippic, p. 122. καὶ ἄτιμος, φησί, τεθνάτω· τοῦτο δὲ λέγει καθαρὸν τὸν τούτων τινὰ ἀποκτείναντα εἶναι.   See too Genesis iv. 14. 'Every one that findeth me shall slay me.'   The *private* blood-revenge of Numbers, c. xxxv., is different.

§ 7.

EXTENSION OF FAMILY LAW TO OFFENCES WITHOUT THE FAMILY.

THE duties, breaches of duty, or offences, as between man and man, which have hitherto been noticed, are all connected with the family or with that relation which the Romans must have regarded as analogous to a family one, from their use of the word *patronus*[a].   The following fragment is of much importance, as shewing not only the origin of criminal justice, but also a great increase in its scope and improvement in its application.

We find in Festus this article:—*Parricidi* quaestores was the name given to officers wont to be created for the investigation of capital offences. For the word *parricida* did not in every case mean such person as had killed a parent but (also him who had killed) any man soever uncondemned. That this was so is shewn by a law of King Numa Pompilius framed in these words: 'If any shall have done (lit. given) to death a free man wittingly and with malicious purpose let him be *paricidas*ᵇ. It is with the latter part of this passage that we have at present to do; postponing consideration of the *quaestors*, whose institution need not necessarily, though it *may*, have been contemporaneous with the enactment of the law.

It is evidently necessary first to determine the exact meaning of *paricida*, which M. Ortolan and Sir Patrick Colquhoun derive in a manner fatal to the conclusions that I venture to think may be drawn from this law. The latter author draws a distinction between *paricide* with one *r* and *parricide* with two, the former from *parem* and *caedo* signifying the murder of an equal, i. e. a fellow-citizen, not a slave; the latter from *patrem* and *caedo* with a 'softening of the *t*,' signifying the murder of a father.

Ortolan attributes to *parricidium* at least the signification of '*paris-cidium*,' without any distinction between the single and double *r*, and translates the word 'meurtre de son semblableᶜ.'

No such distinction as that drawn by Sir P. Colquhoun is to be found, to my knowledge, in any ancient writer. Moreover, if the law be quoted 'verbatim et litteratim,' as the unique retention of a nominative ending in the *a*-declension indicates, the single *r* goes for nothing, double letters not being written before 200 B.C. The invariable length, however, of the first syllable is irreconcileable with a derivation from *par, păris,* especially when we compare *homicida,* where a lost syllable (-*ni*-) might have produced compensatory lengthening, but has not.

The *meaning,* moreover, as given by Ortolan, is too philosophical for an early age, and, as given by Colquhoun, reduces the law to a definition-clause little more than tautological.

The difficulties of the ordinary derivation are considerable. At least I know no instance where, in a Latin word, *t* is assimilated to *r.* On the whole, though the *loss* (of *nt*-) is considerable, I am disposed to trace the word to *parenticida* with a compensatory lengthening of the *a* in *pāricida.* Plautus' comic *perenticida* is an argument for *parenticida* having existed, as there is nothing in *pera* to suggest the *nt.*

Verrius Flaccus is apparently in favour of *parenticida* (non utique is qui *parentem* occidisset). Quinctilian (Inst. 3. 6. 35) of *patricida.*

Mommsen calls these *quaestores* 'trackers of malicious homicide' (Spürer des argen mordes), an expression pointing rather to the *law* quoted by Festus than to any derivational meaning of *Paricida.*

We find in later times the signification of *parricidium* extended to cover many cases of murder between relations but not murder generally[d], and there is, I think, on the whole, little doubt that the old word *paricida* meant strictly murder of a parent.

If this be the case, the law quoted by Festus involves an important step in criminal legislation. This is no definition of an ill-understood term but the application of a well-understood penalty to a new case. It is not necessary that parricide proper should have been a common crime: merely that its prohibition was already recognized

under known sanctions, religious no doubt in origin though
perfectly practical in effect[e]. We have then, probably,
here a type of the origin and growth of criminal law, in
the utilization of a penalty upon homicide *within the
family*, for the prohibition of homicide *within the community*. The words *paricidas esto* do not call a murderer
a parricide, as Plutarch absurdly fancies[f], but, by means of
a legal fiction, treat him as one. That this way of dealing
with murder continued to be intelligible and practical
down to the times of the Republic is shewn by the negative
clause (*parricida ne sit*) in Flaccus' 'first tribunician law'
(§ 6. note o).

As to the manner of enactment of this primitive criminal statute, the procedure under it, the court where such
procedure took place, we are alike destitute of any trustworthy information.

It is clear that no merely family tribunal could have
been competent to deal with offences beyond the pale
of the family ; nor is it likely that the delivery of sentences so much connected with the peace of the community could have been left to a general gathering, or
their execution to Lynch law. *A priori* reasoning would
therefore seem to lead us, in accordance with consistent
tradition, to the king as a permanent *ex officio* judge.
Necessity also must soon have been seen for the appointment of regular subordinate officers to apprehend and
arraign offenders.

a. Festus, *Patr*[onus a patre cur ab antiquis dictus] sit manifestum
quia [ut liberi sic etiam clientes] numerari inter do[mus familiam
quodammodo possunt]. The restorations are those of Müller and
Ursinus. Servius on Aen. 6. 609. Patroni quasi patres.

b. *Parrici*[di] quaestores appellabantur qui solebant creari caussa
rerum capitalium quaerendarum. nam parricida non utique is
qui parentem occidisset dicebatur sed qualemcunque hominem
indemnatum. ita fuisse indicat lex Numae Pompili regis his com-

posita uerbis *si qui hominem liberum dolo sciens morti duit pari-cidas esto.*

Duit is, I think, rightly considered by Schöll to be future per-fect. Compare Festus '*duis* duas habet significationes. nam et pro δίς ponebatur et pro dederis,' and Plautus Amphit. prol. 67 sqq. where *duint* stands in juxtaposition with uiderint, ambisset, ambiuerit.

The very rare *s* as a nominative ending in the first declension has been remarked.

If the translation of *rerum* by *offences* requires justification, see Festus on '*quadriplator* qui…eas res persequerentur quarum ex legibus quadrupli erat actio.' Whether *res* is or is not etymo-logically connected with O. H. G. *racha* (caussa), which Corssen (Beit. 25) denies, this is an unquestionable meaning of the word, from which *reus* surely comes. See Corssen, Ausspr. 1². 477.

c. Colquhoun's Summary of the Roman Civil Law, pt. 1. § 40. Or-tolan, Histoire de la Législation Romaine, § 95. (Explication His-torique, 8me ed.)

d. See Iustin Instt. 4. 18. § 6. on the Lex Pompeia de parricidiis which deals with 'any one that has hastened the death of parent or son or generally of that class of relations which is comprised under the name of parricide.' The list is given by Marcianus, Digest. 48. 9. 1.

e. The traditional punishment, which is described in the last-quoted passage of the Institutes, is stated by Modestinus (Dig. 48. 9. 9. pr.) to have been instituted 'more maiorum,' an expression pointing to at least considerable antiquity. See Dionysius 4. 62, who there makes Tarquinius Superbus sew up in an ox-hide and cast into the sea 'as a parricide' one M. Atilius, a faithless custodian of the Sibylline books. This tallies with Cicero's 'insui in culeum atque in fluuium deici' (pro Sexto Roscio, 25. 26. §§ 70. 73). So too the Auctor ad Herenn. (1. 13. 23) quotes the 'law' under which Mal-leolus suffered as follows: 'qui parentem necasse iudicatus erit ut is obuolutus et obligatus corio deuehatur in profluentem.' This sentence, though inserted sandwich-fashion between two fragments from the Twelve Tables, is, in form at least, clearly of later date. In the passage copied by Cicero (De Iuvent. 2. 50. § 143) from this last, only the fragments from the Twelve Tables occur, though mention is made (§ 149) of certain laws under which the particular criminal suffered this penalty.

Valerius Maximus gives the same story about M. Atilius as that given by Dionysius, adding that the punishment was 'non multo post' (with a variant 'multo post'!) legally enacted for parricide.

Plutarch (Rom. 32) makes L. Hostius 'after the Hannibalian war' the first parricide.

Publicius Malleolus, above-mentioned (a matricide), is said by Florus (Epit. Liv. 68) to have been the first sewn in a leathern sack and flung into the sea.

f. Plutarch, Romulus 32. He evidently refers the law to this hero. Ἴδιον δὲ τὸ μηδεμίαν δίκην κατὰ πατροκτόνων ὁρίσαντα πᾶσαν ἀνδροφο-νίαν πατροκτονίαν προσειπεῖν ὡς τούτου μὲν ὄντος ἐναγοῦς ἐκείνου δὲ ἀδυνάτου.

§ 8.

CRIMES AND WRONGS.   REMISSIBLE PENALTY.

WHATEVER were the penalties involved in the sentence *paricidas esto* there seems no reason to believe that they could be remitted at the option of those most nearly affected by the murder. Otherwise in Horatius' case, to be shortly noticed, the whole machinery of the trial *perduellionis* is unnecessary: the hero might have been at once put upon his trial for murder and discharged, on the father (as the person damnified by his daughter's murder) expressing a wish to waive the charge. The present section will be devoted to other grounds for believing that when the law attributed to Numa (*si quis... paricidas esto*) was passed, the proper distinction had already been drawn between a public and private offence. The inexactness of Blackstone's definition of a crime as differing from a civil injury has been well shewn by Austin from whose 17th lecture (p. 417 ed. 1869) I quote the following passage. 'The difference between crimes and civil injuries is not to be sought for in a supposed difference between their tendencies, but in the difference between the modes wherein they are respectively pursued or wherein the sanction is applied in the two cases. An offence which is pursued at the discretion of the injured party or his representative is a civil injury. An offence which is pursued by the sovereign or by the subordinates of the sovereign is a crime.' If we substitute for 'sovereign, &c.' the words 'any member of the state' we arrive at the definition given in the Institutes of 'Public Suits,' so called 'because, generally speaking, any of the people may prosecute them[a].' *E converso*, in such cases, no private individual can remit the penalty. But a different case was probably recognised by the very same law which we are now considering, in early Roman times; a case where the wrong *was* merely the private concern of the parties suffering it, and the penalty might be remitted at their pleasure. I must premise that the point in question depends partly on an *emendation* though one generally received.

'It was provided,' says Servius, 'in the laws of Numa, that, if any had *unintentionally* killed a man, he should, for the life of the slain man, present to the *agnati* of the latter a ram in public meeting[b]. This passage, though not coming to us with the same internal evidence in its favor as the law quoted by Verrius Flaccus, certainly seems from its subject-matter and language to contain part of a subsequent paragraph of that very law. If so, we have involuntary homicide recognised as an injury merely to the family of the deceased and which might be condoned by them. The formal tender however of compensation must have been made and accepted under circumstances of publicity (*in contione*). Nor does there appear any great anachronism in putting upon *contio* here the interpretation given by Flaccus elsewhere.

'*Contio* signifies a meeting, but only a meeting which is called together by a magistrate or public priest[c].' Possibly we may have here the first trace of a *court* of burgesses held, at least, for purposes of record. Such a

meeting is not to be confounded with the chance spec-
tators who side with this or that disputant in the well-
known Homeric trial-scene[d], before the regular court
(there judicial) is assembled. The *fact*, however, at issue
in the Greek case—the payment or non-payment of compensation for homicide—affords an interesting parallel to
the similar practice of which we have this slight trace in
early Roman times, and which is to be found to a much
greater extent in the infancy of most northern European
nations. It does not follow that the exaction of *blood-
revenge* for murder was allowed among the Romans at any
time of which we have knowledge[e], or, on the other hand,
because no composition is offered in Horatius' case, that
therefore none existed in cases of *involuntary* homicide[f].

It was premised that the main point in this passage—
of compensation for or at least condonation of involuntary
homicide—depended on an emendation. The words translated 'to the agnati of the slain man in public meeting,'
agnatis eius in contione, run in the original '*et natis eius
in cautione.*' The last words, which Schöll appears to
retain (Reliqq. 150), might bear the meaning 'by way of
security,' i.e., for further or other payment, though one
would have expected in *cautionem*. This meaning is by
no means adverse to the general aspect of the transaction,
for the ram is more likely to have been a mere earnest or
formal tender than an actual compensation. The words
et natis appear to me totally unintelligible here, and may
have arisen very easily from *agnatis* through *ac natis*.
The verb *offerre*, too, used by Servius, indicates a presen-
tation or tender to some human being, and is therefore in
favor of *agnatis*. The absolute sense of *offering* a victim
(to Heaven understood) is late, or at least not Servian.

The view then here taken of involuntary homicide as
a private injury, condonable by those interested, seems

clearly made out. That the transaction took place under religious auspices is highly probable; the 'public priest,' who could call the *contio*, would doubtless preside over it. And, as the wrath of heaven as well as that of man had to be appeased, the earnest of compensation might well become the vicarious victim or purificatory sacrifice. This meaning, though foreign to *offerre,* may be gathered from other expressions of Servius as well as of Flaccus[a]. The Athenian law tallied in both points with the Roman; the homicide must be purified, but he must first get the consent of the slain man's relatives[b].

Finally, it should not be overlooked that in the ancient fragment (si quis...*dolo sciens*...) preserved by Flaccus, and its probable sequel (si quis...*imprudens*...) paraphrased by Servius, we have not only a real distinction drawn between crimes and wrongs, but a clear definition of murder as characterised by that malice prepense which still constitutes the grand criterion of the same crime in our own common law. The same distinction and the same procedure in case of involuntary homicide was preserved by the Twelve Tables. 'To fling a weapon,' says Cicero, 'is a matter of intent; to hit the man whom you do not wish to hit, a matter of chance. Hence the substitution (perhaps 'vicarious slaughter') of that ram in your legal proceedings, *if a man's weapon hath flown from his hand rather than he hath flung it*[i].' The italicised words are quoted by the same author elsewhere[j], as a law of the Twelve Tables. The coincidence in kind of the Roman vicarious sacrifice with that mentioned in Genesis xxii. 13, though curious, can scarce be more than accidental.

---

a. Iustin. Instt. 4. 18. 1. Publica iudicia dicta sunt quod cuiuis ex populo executio eorum plerumque datur.

b. Servius on *ipse...aries* Ecl. 4. 43. Sane in Numae legibus cautum

R. L.   D

est ut si quis imprudens occidisset hominem pro capite occisi agnatis eius in contione offerret arietem.

c. Festus s.v. *contio.*

d. Homer, Iliad, 19. 497—508.

e. Mommsen, Hist. 1. 11. (p. 158. n. tr.)

f. as Zumpt argues Absch. 1. Cap. 9. p. 127.

g. Servius on another *ipse aries* Geor. 3. 387. bene *ipse* addit, quasi qui aut dominus gregis est aut qui contra pro domino capital dari consuenerat. nam apud maiores homicidi poenam noxius arietis damno luebat, quod in regum legibus legitur. The passage in Festus is mutilated, but may be restored with tolerable certainty *Subici* ar[ies dicitur qui pro occiso datur] quod fit ut ait Cincius [in libro de officio iuris-]-consulti exemplo At-[-hamantis ex quo *or* -heniensium apud quos] expiandi gratia aries in-[-igitur ab eo qui inuitus sce-]-lus admisit, poenae p[endendae loco]. For Müller's *inigitur* Mercklin reads *m-actatur. inigitur* seems the better on account of the following passage in Festus. *Subigere* arietem Antistius esse ait dare arietem qui pro se agatur caedatur. The last explanation is doubtless correct, *sub* as usual in composition meaning substitution, and *subigi* to be led as a substitute for one's self, being written *subici* from the old unity of symbol for c and g and after confused with a compound of *icere* or *iacere* (see note *i.*)

h. Demosthenes c. Aristoc. 643. 4. τί οὖν ὁ νόμος κελεύει; τὸν ἁλόντα ἐπ᾽ ἀκουσίῳ φόνῳ...φεύγειν ἕως ἂν αἰδέσηταί τις τῶν ἐν γένει τοῦ πεπονθότος τηνικαῦτα δ᾽ ἥκειν δέδωκεν ἔστιν ὃν τρόπον--οὐχ ὃν ἂν τύχῃ--ἀλλὰ καὶ θῦσαι κ.τ.λ. εἴρηκεν ἃ χρὴ ποιῆσαι.

There is an interesting variant αἰδέσηταί τινα recognised by Harpocration (Αἰδέσασθαι... ἐν τῷ κατ᾽ Ἀριστοκράτους ἀντὶ τοῦ ἐξιλάσασθαι καὶ πεῖσαι) which might perhaps mean (like ἐπιθαυμάζειν, Aristoph. Nubes 1117) to compliment by a present. The law, however, quoted by Dem. adv. Macartatus is in favour of the construction *first* given above.

i. Cicero Topica 17. 64. nam iacere telum uoluntatis est, ferire quem nolueris fortunae. ex quo aries ille subiicitur in uestris actionibus *si telum manu fugit magis quam iecit.*

j. pro Tullio 21. 51. Lex est in xii tabulis *si telum manu fugit magis quam iecit.*

§ 9.

CRIMES AND WRONGS. FEW PROPERTY OFFENCES.

IT does not of course follow, from the fact of a distinction having been drawn between crimes and wrongs, that particular offences were classed under the one head or the other exactly as we should class them. In fact it is more than doubtful whether at the early period we are considering, the law yet took cognisance of civil injuries as exclusively matters for compensation at all. Only, a number of actions being recognised as *prima facie* penal (and that most likely at first because violations of divine law), it was understood that the penalty might in some cases be remitted by private persons and in other cases not. The religious origin of Roman law produces a curious result in the way in which most offences against property and many against the person are treated. Not only cases of ordinary theft but even robbery and assault, all of which are of course with modern nations matter for indictment, were not so with the Romans, but simply constituted an obligation *ex delicto* which might or might not be enforced at the pure option of the sufferer alone. The reason probably is that these offences did not attract legislative notice until the time was past for identifying them with breaches of religious duty. The difficulty of such identification is doubtless one reason for the paucity in early legislation of rules relating to property. Another is that which is alleged by Mr Maine in the 10th chapter of *Ancient Law*, and which is specially applicable to Rome—the small proportionate number, in an infant community, of persons between whom any dispute as to property could arise. There could be neither offence nor contested claim between members of a family as to goods or lands which were in the eye of the law exclusively owned by the head. Accordingly the few property offences noticed by regal law are encroachments upon the family inheritance as a whole, or its produce : and these, it must be remarked, are not treated, in accordance with the spirit of later legislation, as subjects for civil action but as *crimes*, prohibited by religious sanctions of the usual tremendous kind.

Such is the enactment attributed to Numa that he who ploughed up a landmark should be devoted to the gods, himself and his oxen[a]. Examples will at once occur, from the Old Testament, of the same feeling of sanctity attached to boundaries and to patrimony generally[b]. It is possible moreover that the lands of a *gens*, which no doubt lay together, were divided into family portions by no more substantial boundaries than the imaginary lines drawn from post to post, which still with us often serve to divide small holdings of garden-ground : in which case the boundary stone assumes an importance scarcely intelligible to the owners of fenced and hedged estates.

With this boundary law may be ranked, in the character of its sanction and probably in the antiquity of its origin, an enactment of the Twelve Tables against nocturnal theft ; in the latter point, one against the charming away of a neighbour's crop. Whoever should have been guilty of the second offence was liable doubtless to some penalty, but what, Pliny does not tell us[c]. The offence of grazing or cutting a crop on arable land by night was anciently capital, the culprit being hung up as a victim to the goddess of harvest, and so slain : a mitigation of this law in the case of juvenile delinquents is, from mention of the praetor, probably later[d]. The supposition, indeed, of a date prior to the Twelve Tables for the two last-mentioned enactments is a mere supposition, dependent on subject-matter and the archaic character of the sanction. Nor have we even this last reason for referring to the regal period the laws punishing an incendiary with burning and a false witness with hurling from the Tarpeian rock; though there is certainly ground for attributing high antiquity to them if not, with Mommsen, royal origin[e].

a. Festus: *Termino* sacra faciebant quod in eius tutela fines agrorum esse putabant. denique Numa Pompilius statuit eum qui terminum exarasset et ipsum et boues sacros esse.

   Dionysius Antiqq. 2. 74. εἰ δέ τις ἀφανίσειεν ἢ μεταθείη τοὺς ὅρους ἱερὸν ἐνομοθέτησεν (ὁ Νομᾶς) εἶναι τῷ θεῷ (Διὶ ὁρίῳ) τὸν τούτων τι διαπραξάμενον, ἵνα τῷ βουλομένῳ κτείνειν αὐτὸν ὡς ἱερόσυλον ἥ τε ἀσφάλεια καὶ τὸ καθαρὸν μιάσματος εἶναι προσῇ.

b. Deuteronomy xix. 14: xxvii. 17. Ruth iv. 3–8. Numbers xxxvi. 7. 1 Kings xxi. 3. &c.

c. Pliny Hist. Nat. 28. 4. 17. Quid? non et legum ipsarum in xii tabulis uerba sunt *qui fruges excantassit.* See Servius on Ecl. 8. 29 (atque satas alio uidi traducere messes) magicis quibusdam artibus hoc fiebat. unde est in xii tabulis *neue alienam segetem pellexeris* quod et Varro et multi scriptores fieri deprehensum animaduertunt. The alleged fragment from Seruius is, in spite of the technical-looking word *pellicere*, justly regarded with suspicion by Schöll (Reliqq. 49) because of the use of the *second* person in the prohibition and the conjunctive for the imperative mood.

d. Pliny H. N. 18. 3. 12. Frugem quidem aratro quaesitam furtim noctu pauisse ac secuisse puberi xii tabulis capital erat suspensumque Cereri necari iubebant grauius quam in homicidio conuictum: impubem praetoris arbitratu uerberari noxiamue duplionemue decerni.

   noxiam decerni most probably means an order for the giving-up of the delinquent to the person aggrieved.

e. Mommsen Hist. 1. 11. p. 158 tr. The punishment of the incendiary is quoted Dig. 47. 9. 9. from Gaius on the Twelve Tables: but there is nothing in the quotation to shew that the law comes from them.

   The punishment is said to have been retained in later times. So Callistratus in Dig. 48. 19. 28. 12.

   The passage in Aulus Gellius' Attic Nights, which is our authority for the punishment of false witness, seems rather to place it *before* the time of the Twelve Tables. 20. 1. 53.

An putas, Fauorine, si non illa *etiam* ex xii tabulis de testimoniis falsis poena aboleuisset et si nunc quoque ut antea, qui falsum testimonium dixisse conuictus esset, e saxo Tarpeio deiiceretur, mentituros fuisse pro testimonio tam multos quam uidemus? The word *etiam* indicates, I think, a different and milder penalty in the Twelve Tables.

§ 10.

Early Legislature and Judicature. Kings. Pontiffs.

In the so-called laws hitherto cited whether we consider duty, offence or sanction, as also in the oldest customs of the Roman people, a religious origin is apparent. It is, in fact, this prevailing, religious character, which, coupled with the reverent retention of very old linguistic forms, seems to justify us in dating these fragments before those of the Twelve Tables. A slight degree of weight may also be given to the names with which the former are traditionally connected. But of their regular enactment by a civil authority, as of the procedure under them and the execution of their sentences, we know next to nothing. Our historical authorities refer the first Roman laws as well as the oldest Roman customs, civil or religious, to one or other of the well-known kings. These may possibly have been real persons, with the exception of Romulus, who is a mere eponymous hero. A Numa, Tullus, and Ancus *may* have been actual chieftains of the Pomponii, Hostilii, and Marcii, who afterwards claimed them as ancestors". As to the author of the Servian reform, there is such a uniform persistent and peculiar character in the traditions and usages connected with him, that it is difficult to avoid believing him to be a real person, in spite of the miraculous stories clearly arising from his first name. The sovereignty of the Tarquinian family, their oppressive rule and total expulsion have never been successfully called in question.

As a record, however, of actual facts, it has now come to be generally agreed that the history of the regal period possesses little value. It is sufficient here to refer to the continual admixture of the supernatural element and to the unparalleled average length of the reigns. And this was not a hereditary monarchy where a king may ascend the throne very young, like George the third of England and Lewis the fourteenth of France. Each king of Rome must have at least attained early manhood before royalty, and moreover the career of these wonderful men was in four cases cut short by a violent death and in one by deposition[b].

The facts, however, narrated by the historians of the regal period, may, where they involve any legal or constitutional point, have some value as typically though not actually true. They will at least be likely to have been invented in accordance with what was believed to be ancient practice. The some remark applies to general statements of old constitutional principles. And if we find that our conclusions drawn from these grounds tally with what is, though scanty, the best evidence of all—the formulas and customs preserved by antiquarians—we may perhaps hope that we have attained something like truth.

The legislative power—at least that of *proposing* laws —is generally represented as vested in the king, the senate being merely a body of advisers chosen at the king's pleasure, while the function of the burgess-assembly (in this respect) is restricted to the ratification of laws which the king prepares and propounds[c].

We should rather have been disposed, from the character of the earliest laws, to attribute them to the *pontiffs*,
whom on other grounds we know to have exercised powers
and discharged duties of secular as well as religious
importance.

We have seen how their superintendence of the gentile
sacra gave them the control of the important business of
arrogation. They had the management of the Calendar
with all the political influence flowing from exclusive
knowledge of the times when public business could properly be transacted. It seems strange at first sight to
find these depositories of sacred lore overseers of *works* as
well as days. But they were undoubtedly from time immemorial connected with the construction and repair of
the bridge which formed the communication between
Rome and the Gate fortress (Ianiculum) on the Etrurian
side[d]. On Mommsen's hypothesis, that *pons* in this word
means not merely 'bridge,' but, according to the most
probable etymology, 'way' generally (Curtius, Grundzüge
pa. 253), the occurrence of pontiffs in other old Latin
communities *not* connected with any river is explained,
and the great importance is evident of an office which
superintended the means of communication between the
originally detached clan-settlements[e].

The author first quoted recognizes the great part which
these authorities played in early Rome, attributing to
them, among other things, the fixing and promulgating of
'the general exoteric precepts of ritual which were known
under the name of the *royal laws.*' A similar conclusion
drawn from the originally religious character of these laws
has been hinted at above; but their subsequent developement and application must be ignored before they can be
barely described as 'precepts of ritual.'

Whether the complexion of the first laws came merely

from the influence of the pontiffs with the king or whether, as I believe, the regal power itself was in its remote origin a developement of the pontifical, I must leave to the reader's decision[f].

As to the carrying out of law, the old authorities in general attribute supreme judicial and executive power to the king: such power if occurring in other hands is only either permitted or delegated by him. Thus Diony-sius tells us that it was part of Romulus' prerogative to decide upon the most serious cases himself while he en-trusted the minor ones to his senators[g]; Pomponius, that, as to magistracy the kings had, in the commencement of the Roman polity, the whole power, &c. &c.[h].

The above and similar passages prove a received tra-dition of respectable antiquity, borne out to some extent by what we know in more historical times of the dictator-ship, an office which the Romans regarded as closely resembling the kingly. It is not however so much from general statements about the early constitution of Rome that we derive our most trustworthy information as from slight references to practice—the safest perhaps when un-designed—in the accounts of early cases. Of these, what have been reported by the historians are of course only such as were remarkable for some matter of great public interest. To us, they have a different value as preserving relics of ordinary practice; and, in this point of view, the legendary character of the facts is of little moment, pro-vided the legend be old. Such is Livy's account of the trial of the surviving and victorious Horatius for his sister's murder[i].

Whether we consider the whole story of the Horatii as a fiction or not, it is clear that the latter part contains the facts and formulæ of a very old procedure referred by our best historical authority to the first century of Rome's

existence. The narrative of the punishment of Mettius, on
the other hand, contains no remnant of antiquity, and
would, moreover, constitute, at best, merely an instance of
military imperium.

a. NVM. POMPIL. is read in the exergue of a denarius figured by
Patin. Obverse L. POMPON. MOLO. This, however, being an
equestrian family is not likely to have belonged to the old aristocracy. Pavor and Pallor, to whom Tullus vows a temple (Livy
1. 27) are supposed to be represented on denarii of L. Hostilius
Saserna. On both brass and silver coins of L. Marcius Censorinus
appear heads of Numa and Ancus. (The latter was said to be the
son of Numa Marcius by Pompilia, daughter of king Numa.)

b. Dionysius (Antiqq. 1. 75) soberly reckons up the years of the
seven reigns. The total is 244. Even the utterly improbable
supposition of a year of 10 months during the whole of the regal
period only reduces the number to 203. This is within 7 years of
the first seven kings of Judah who begin with three reigns of 48,
31 and 40 years, and are moreover hereditary after the first two
reigns. The tremendous reigns of Lewis the fourteenth and
fifteenth of France only raise the number of years from the ac-
cession of Charles the ninth to the execution of Lewis the sixteenth
to 233 years. There are here three violent deaths, though not of
young men: but it must be remembered that the monarchy was
hereditary and of the two princes first mentioned the one ascended
the throne at 5 and the other at 15 years of age. No selection of
consecutive reigns in English history comes to any thing like
even this.

c. Dionysius Antiqq. 2. 14. τῷ δὲ δημοτικῷ πλήθει τρία ταῦτα (ὁ
Ῥωμύλος) ἐπέτρεψεν ἀρχαιρεσιάζειν τε καὶ νόμους ἐπικυροῦν καὶ περὶ
πολέμου διαγιγνώσκειν ὅταν ὁ βασιλεὺς ἐφῇ, see too 4. 13. Tacitus
Ann. 3. 26. Nobis Romulus ut libitum imperitaverat: dein Numa
religionibus et diuino iure populum deuinxit, repertaque quaedam
a Tullo et Anco, sed praecipuos Seruius Tullius sanctor legum fuit
quis etiam reges obtemperarent. The last words point of course
to a narrowing of the royal power which will be noticed hereafter.
Zumpt argues very strongly for a narrowing of the royal legislative
power from the earliest times by the necessity for consent on the
part of the comitia curiata, Erster Absch. Cap. 2. He relies
mainly upon passages of Dionysius such as that above quoted,
4. 13. τοὺς νόμους (ὁ Τούλλιος) ... ἐκύρωσε ταῖς φράτραις &c., and upon

Pomponius (Dig. 1. 2. 2. 2), leges (Romulus)...curiatas ad populum *tulit. tulerunt* et sequentes reges.

d. Festus. *Ianiculum* dictum quod per eum Romanus populus primitus transierit in agrum Etruscum. The road lay in the reverse direction to Porsena : and it was doubtless originally for the security of Rome that this bridge was always to be of wood and easily destructible. Dionysius Antiqq. 3. 45. καὶ τὴν ξυλίνην γέφυραν ἣν ἄνευ χαλκοῦ καὶ σιδήρου θέμις ὑπ' αὐτῶν διακρατεῖσθαι τῶν ξύλων ἐκεῖνος (ὁ Ἄγκος) ἐπιθεῖναι τῷ Τιβέρει λέγεται ἣν ἄχρι τοῦ παρόντος διαφυλάττουσιν ἱερὰν εἶναι νομίζοντες. εἰ δέ τι πονήσειεν αὐτῆς μέρος οἱ ἱεροφάνται θεραπεύουσι.

The mutilated words in Festus (s. v. *Sublicium*) ne inrumpendi p. (for inrumiendi) sublicibus cauata...are, as it seems to me, more likely to have been p[otestas sit] than (as Müller) p[ontis sublici].

e. Dr Donaldson gives a strange meaning to pons (a weight laid down) in pontifex, holding this word to describe 'the functions of the priest who settled the atonement for a specific fault by the imposition of a fine &c. &c.' Varronianus 13 § 9. Varro's derivation is surely safer, 'ego a ponte arbitror, nam ab his (pontificibus) sublicius est factus primum ut restitutus saepe, cum in eo sacra et uls et cis Tiberim non mediocri ritu fiant.

The passage in Mommsen is 1. 12. (pp. 178, 9 of tr.) The pontiffs might not ride on horseback but only in a carriage. Could this have been meant to bring the state of the roads home to them ? See, for the fact, a magnificent specimen of Servius, (on *exsortem* Aen. 8. 552,) accounting for the apparently unclerical conduct of Aeneas, who is well known to have been a pontiff.

f. The tradition about the typical prince Aeneas is really somewhat in point. More so, is the retention, in republican times, of the proscribed title *rex* in connection with the *sacra* alone, see Dionysius Antiqq. 5. 1. Livy's account clearly contains some truth. Et quia quaedam publica sacra per ipsos reges factitata erant... regem sacrificulum creant (primi consules) 2. 2. id sacerdotium, adds Livy, pontifici subiecere, differing from Flaccus who gives the order (s. v. *Ordo*) thus. Rex, Flamen Dialis, Flamen Martialis, Flamen Quirinalis, Pontifex Maximus. The cognomina Rex and Regulus may have indicated tradition of sacerdotal functions. The former was borne by a (plebeian ?) branch of the Marcii, the alleged descendants of Numa and Ancus : the latter by a branch, also said to be plebeian, of the Atilii, one of whom is made out, it will be remembered, by Dionysius to have been a custodian of the Sibylline books. Reginus, a cognomen of the Antistii, may perhaps have a local meaning. It is unnecessary to quote instances, from other nations, of the connection and frequent identity of king and priest in early times, which is one of the commonplaces of history.

g.   Antiqq. 2. 14. βασιλεῖ μὲν οὖν ἐξῄρητο τάδε τὰ γέρα ... τῶν ἀδικη- μάτων τὰ μέγιστα μὲν αὐτὸν δικάζειν τὰ δὲ ἐλάττονα τοῖς βουλευταῖς ἐπιτρέπειν. See also 2. 29.

h.   Digest. 1. 2. 1. 14.

i.   Livy, 2. 23.

§ 11.

THE STORY OF HORATIUS.

THE part of the story with which we are concerned commences with Horatius being *raptus in ius* (the regular phrase of a later period) *ad regem*—haled off to the king's court. If any stress is to be laid upon this expression it must almost imply the existence of regular police officers, for who else would be likely to arrest Horatius? Scarcely the people who afterwards acquit him[a]: certainly not the king, who shuns the odium of such a trial and actually suggests a way of escape to the accused. If there were such officers in the time at which the story is placed, they would in all probability be the *quaestores parricidi* before mentioned—the 'trackers of murder' not to be identified with the *duumviri*, but, according to Mommsen's correct view, "standing deputies, whose primary duty was to search for and arrest murderers, and who therefore acted as a sort of police[b]." To proceed, however, with the story. "The king, to avoid giving his personal sanction to a sentence so sad and so unpopular, or to an execution in pursuance of such sentence, summoning an assembly of the people, says: I create, according to law, two commissioners to decide the charge of *perduellio*

in the case of Horatius. This law was one of direful
strain[c]. 'Let the two commissioners decide the charge of
perduellio. If he (the accused) shall have appealed from
them, let him contest the case with them on the appeal.
If they shall prevail, veil his head, hang him by a rope to
a barren tree[d], scourge him either within or without the
pomoerium.' Accordingly, when the commissioners created
under this law, who did not consider themselves competent,
under the law, to acquit even a guiltless homicide, had
found Horatius guilty, 'Horatius,' says one of them, 'I
decide the charge of *perduellio* against thee. Go, lictor,
bind his hands.' The lictor had approached and was
casting on the noose. Then Horatius, at the instance of
Tullus, a merciful interpreter of the law, says ' I appeal.'
So the case was contested on the appeal before the people."

Then follow the speech of the father Horatius at the
historical Horatian Trophy; the acquittal of the son, con-
ditioned on the expiation of his blood-guiltiness at the
public cost; the institution of the traditional purificatory
rites of the Horatian gens; and the erection of the Sister's
Beam, ever after repaired at the national expense, beneath
which the brother is sent, with veiled head, in nominal
execution of the first sentence.

With the origin of the legend, as a matter of fact, I
have not here to do, so that I need not pause to trace the
three Roman champions (as possibly the three later defenders of the bridge), to some surname of the Horatian
family; nor the rest of the story to the peculiar Horatian
sacra, the Horatian pillar, and the Tigillum Sororium,
under the title of which last another account appears in
Festus[e]. Whether founded in fact or not, the *narrative* has
too poetical and dramatic a form to be much relied upon for
our present purpose. It is different with the professed
quotation, the antiquity of which there seems no reason

to doubt. From this we gather the existence in the regal period of a commission to try *perduellio*, an appeal from the commissioners' decision, and a definite public penalty assigned in case of that decision being supported. For all else we have to depend upon the statements of later historians and orators, and the illustrations afforded by subsequent practice. The latter class of authorities will be noticed as they apply; to the former belong the account of Livy given above, that of Flaccus[*], and one by Dionysius which is appended hereto[f].

a. Dionysius (Antiqq. 3. 22) καγε προσέρχονται (τῷ βασιλεῖ) τῶν πολιτικῶν ἄνδρες οὐκ ἀφανεῖς τὸν Ὁράτιον ἄγοντες ὑπὸ δίκην.

b. Mommsen Hist. 1. ch. 11 (p. 159 tr.). See generally below § 18.

c. Dr Donaldson, who detects the Saturnian metre in this formula, apparently gives *carmen* what is generally conceived to be its original sense. This, however, is *not* necessarily connected with tune or metre, as the word cannot, in accordance with analogy, be derived from cano, though, of course, connected with Camena (Casmena). (See Corssen Ausspr. 1². 605 n.). Carmen is more probably used here merely in the sense of a repeated or recurring form of words. Compare, inter alia, Livy 3. 64. recitabat rogationis carmen and Raschig's note on 1. 24 and 26 of the same author Carmen omnis sollemnis formula appellatur.

d. Festus. *Felices* arbores Cato dixit quae fructum ferunt, *infelices* quae non ferunt. So, too, the word is used by Livy 5. 24. Macrobius (Saturn. 3. 20) seems to make *infelices* out to be black-fruited trees.

e. Festus. *sororium* tigillum appellatur hac de caussa. ex conuentione Tulli Hostili regis et Metti Fufiti ducis Albanorum trigemini Horatii et Curiatii cum dimicassent, ut uictores sequeretur imperium, et Horatius noster exsuperasset uictorque domum reuerteretur, obuia soror cognita morte sponsi, sui fratris manu occisi, auersata est eius osculum, quo nomine Horatius interficit eam et quanquam a patre absolutus sceleris erat accusatus tamen parricidi apud Duumuiros, damnatusque prouocauit ad populum, cuius iudicio uictor, duo tigilla tertio supericecto, quae pater eius constituerat, uelut sub iugum missus subit, consecratisque ibi aris **Iunoni Sororiae et Iano Curiatio liberatus** omni noxia sceleris est auguriis adprobantibus, ex quo sororium id tigillum est appellatum.

Dionysius 3. 21 mentions the two altars still remaining in his time built apparently into the opposite house-walls of a narrow street, the beam being let into the walls above;—in the forum, an angular pillar on which the spoils of the Curiatii had been fixed. The spoils have disappeared, says Dionysius naively, through length of time, but the pillar preserves its title of 'the Horatian.'

f. Dionysius 3. 22. The part relating to the trial.

προσέρχονται (τῷ βασιλεῖ) τῶν πολιτικῶν ἀνδρῶν οὐκ ἀφανεῖς τὸν Ὁράτιον ἄγοντες ὑπὸ δίκην ὡς οὐ καθαρὸν αἵματος ἐμφυλίου διὰ τὸν τῆς ἀδελφῆς φόνον...τοὺς νόμους παρεχόμενοι τοὺς οὐκ ἐῶντας ἄκριτον ἀποκτείνειν οὐδένα καὶ τὰ παρὰ τῶν θεῶν μηνίματα...διεξιόντες. ὁ δὲ πατὴρ ἀπελογεῖτο...τιμωρίαν οὐ φόνον εἶναι τὸ πραχθὲν λέγων, δικαστήν τε αὑτὸν ἀξιῶν εἶναι τῶν ἰδίων κακῶν ἀμφοτέρων γενόμενον πατέρα... πολλὴ τὸν βασιλέα κατεῖχεν ἀμηχανία...ἄλλως τε καὶ τοῦ πάτρος αὐτὸν ἀπολύοντος τῆς αἰτίας ᾧ τὴν περὶ τῆς θυγατρὸς ὀργὴν ἥ τε φύσις ἀπεδίδου πρώτῳ καὶ ὁ νόμος...τελευτῶν κράτιστον εἶναι διέγνω τῷ δήμῳ τὴν διάγνωσιν ἐπιτρέπειν. γενόμενος δὲ θανατηφόρου κρίσεως τότε πρῶτον ὁ Ῥωμαίων δῆμος κύριος ἀπολύει τοῦ φόνου τὸν ἄνδρα.

§ 12.

THE DUUMVIRI.

IT is not clear from the *quoted* words *duumuiri...iudicent* of Livy or the statement *accusatus...apud duumuiros* of Festus, whether this was a standing court or an extraordinary commission. But the latter is certainly intended by the *narrative* of Livy. And this fact is borne out by the indications, slight as they are, to be found in subsequent practice. In one account of the condemnation of Manlius *duumuiri* are "created to investigate the case of *perduellio*[2]," an expression which could scarcely have been used of a standing tribunal. In Rabirius' case the appointment must have been special, for it is stigmatized as irregular, and made with a hostile intent against the particular defendant[b].

We may then assume the *duumuiri* to have been specially appointed. Their appointment in the case of Horatius would appear, at first sight of Livy's words, to have been the sole act of the king. Zumpt, however, gives very good reasons for believing that the king merely gives the power of electing and that the *duumuiri* are actually elected by the assembly, i. e. the *comitia curiata*, with which he, I think correctly, identifies Livy's *concilium populi aduocatum*[c]. This view, also, accords perfectly with the words *secundum legem facio*, if those words refer to a previously existing enactment which probably specified the manner of creation of the *duumuiri* as well as the procedure to be followed after their creation. An entirely different view is taken of these words by the high modern authority just cited, from whom I have the misfortune, on this last point, to differ *toto caelo*.

Cicero refers to the formal words quoted here by Livy, when addressing the accuser of Rabirius,—"Those words, which so charm *your* merciful and *popular* taste, 'Go, lictor, bind the hands.' are not only no words of our present freedom and humanity, but they are none even of Romulus' or Numa's. To Tarquinius, proudest and cruellest of Kings, belong those formularies of torture, which you, in your mild and popular disposition, repeat with such unction. 'Veil his head—hang him to a barren tree,'—words, gentlemen, long ago obscured not alone by the shades of antiquity but also by the light of liberty[d]." Dr Donaldson took these words to shew that Cicero referred the law to the legislation of Tarquinius[e]. Zumpt, in his note 69, p. 423, takes a somewhat similar view, supposing Cicero to have confused the imposition of a different punishment by this *lex* with the reputed institution of tying to the stake and flogging with rods by Tarquinius[a]. This interpretation of the passage is quite tenable and consistent with the historical inaccuracies found elsewhere in Cicero's works. To myself it seems easier to take the whole passage as an oratorical flourish, meaning that, though this enactment was perhaps attributed to Romulus or Numa, its spirit was much better suited to Tarquinius, the proud and cruel. But the very last inference one would have thought of drawing from Cicero's language is that the *lex* was enacted by Tullus. This is, however, the inference of Zumpt, whereupon is based a great part of the arguments from which he ultimately concludes that the *lex* mentioned by Livy was merely the commission given by the king to the *duumuiri*, answering, in fact, somewhat to the Praetor's formula of later days[g]. It is scarce necessary to go into these arguments, because the position of the words *secundum legem* appears fatal to the conclusion drawn. Had these words belonged to *iudicent* they must surely have stood before it: where they do stand, they can only refer to *facio*; and *secundum legem facio*, 'I make in accordance with law,' must mean in accordance with a law previously existing. We should not gather from Livy's account that the law obliged the king to appoint this commission; merely that it specified the manner of such appointment, if made, and the subsequent procedure.

a. Livy 6. 20.

b. Dio Cassius (xxxvii. 27) says of these commissioners in that case κατεψηφίσαντο αὐτοῦ καίτοι μὴ πρὸς τοῦ δήμου κατὰ τὰ πάτρια, ἀλλὰ πρὸς αὐτοῦ τοῦ στρατηγοῦ οὐκ ἐξὸν αἱρεθέντες.

c. Criminal-recht Absch. 1. Cap. 7. pp. 92, 3. Anmerk. 54. p. 419.

d. Cic. pro Rabirio 4. § 13.

e. Varronianus 6. § 5.

f. Dio Cassius xxiii. fr. 4.

g. Absch. 1. cap. 7. p. 95.

R. L.   E

§ 13.

The Right of Appeal.

THE next point to be noticed is the *appeal.* That this was to the *people*, (i. e. at the time in question, to the *comitia curiata*,) is a fact which, being supported by the later use of the word *prouocatio*, may fairly be believed on the testimony of Livy, Festus, and Cicero[a].

In neither of the two former writers is there any hint at restriction upon the right of appeal, unless this is to be gathered from Livy's expression *auctore Tullo.* The strict technical meaning of these words is perhaps rather *with the sanction* than *at the instance* of Tullus; and a permission which had to be granted might be refused. So too *clemente legis interprete* possibly means that it lay with the king to decide whether the law allowed an appeal or not, in such a case as the present one. (See, however, end of § 16.)

Such an interpretation is quite compatible with the view that the *duumuiri* were elected by the assembly of burgesses, but that it lay in the king's option whether he would call together the assembly for that purpose or not. If they were, on the other hand, the king's mere delegates, not simply appointed but selected at his own will and pleasure, an appeal, as of right, from them to the assembly clearly limits the king's supposed supreme judicial authority. And that this was the view maintained in some traditional account of the affair of Horatius may appear from the words represented by Livy to have been addressed to the dictator Papirius by the old M. Fabius A.V.C. 430. "I will see whether thou wilt yield to that appeal to which the king of Rome, Tullus Hostilius, yielded[b]. These words, while they imply that the *right* of appeal was a moot point, imply also that this was regarded as being virtually an appeal against the king himself. They do not appear to me capable of the construction which Zumpt puts on them, that this was the first case of appeal. The lax flourish of Cicero[a] would prove that this was the first case of a capital sentence at all: unless we are to put, in a purely oratorical passage, upon the word *iudicium* the technical and (here) forced meaning of sentence by *iudices* to whom the magistrate has referred the case, as distinguished from sentence by that magistrate himself. Dionysius (above § 11 note f) expressly represents this as the first appeal. The point now in question, however, is whether appeal was allowed as of right in the regal period, not at what date of that period it became established.

Valerius Maximus expressly states that Horatius, after being condemned by King Tullus, was, on appeal to the people, acquitted[c]. And Cicero, in one passage, maintains, on the authority of the pontifical books, that appeal was allowed even from the kings, which is scarcely reconcileable with the view that the king could limit the right of appeal from the *duumuiri*, whether these were merely his delegates or no[d].

Lastly, the idea that the *duumuiri* could be allowed to give a final sentence seems unreasonable in the face of that limitation of their functions which is clearly implied in Livy's words:—'who did not consider themselves competent under that law, to acquit even a guiltless homicide.' That is, (as Gruter long ago saw,) who held that a mere finding of *fact* fell within their province, not a consideration of extenuating circumstances. Zumpt accepts this as the result of the *lex*, though he takes the latter to be only the special commission of Tullus for the particular case[e].

a. Cicero pro Milone, c. 3. In qua tandem urbe hoc homines stultissimi disputant? nempe in ea quae primum iudicium de capite uidit M. Horati...qui nondum libera ciuitate tamen populi Romani comitiis liberatus est. Livy 1. 26. Certatum ad populum est. Festus. l. c. prouocauit ad populum.

b. Livy 8. 33. Videro cessurusne prouocatione sis cui rex Romanus Tullus Hostilius cessit.

c. Valerius Maximus 8. 1. Absoluti 1. M. Horatius interfectae sororis crimine a Tullo rege damnatus, ad populum prouocato [? iudicio] absolutus est.

I do not set much store by the evidence of this gossiping writer. His date is fixed by a dedication to Tiberius, of sufficiently nauseous character. 'Cetera diuinitas opinione colligitur, tua praesenti fide paterno auitoque sideri par uidetur... &c.'

d. Cic. de Rep. 2. 31 § 54. Prouocationem autem etiam a regibus fuisse declarant pontificii libri significant nostri etiam augurales.

e. Criminal-recht Absch. 1. Cap. 7. p. 97.

§ 14.

The King's supreme Judicial Power.

Some of these passages undoubtedly make against the generally received opinion of the royal judicial authority as supreme in all cases. On the same side may be reckoned Cicero's description of the changes introduced on the expulsion of the Tarquins. "Then came," says Scipio in the dialogue De Republica, "appeals in *every case,*" words certainly capable of the interpretation that appeals had existed before, at least in some cases[a]. Dionysius represents the kings as availing themselves in their judicial capacity of the services of the senators as delegates or counsellors[b], and Livy blames Tarquinius Superbus for neglecting, in capital cases, to consult such a consilium[c] (which Zumpt identifies with that of the judicial functionaries under the republic[d]); but none of the passages in the last two authors go so far as to make out a court of appeal or even of concurrent jurisdiction.

On the other side: Cicero himself compares the authority of a king with the *imperium* of a dictator in time of war[e], from which it is certain that no appeal lay[f]. And Pomponius makes appeal from capital sentences the limitation of consular as distinguished from regal power[g]. The power of the dictator, without special reference to war, is said by Cicero to be nearest to the likeness of the royal[h]. This remark is made of T. Lartius, the first dictator, whose appointment, says Livy, was so formidable to the plebeians because there was no appeal from him[i]. The question, however, of appeal under the republic does not properly arise here.

Dionysius, in the case of Horatius, makes it apparently, an entirely voluntary action of the king to refer the matter to the people[j]. This is in accordance with the other passages in the same author, which leave the supreme judicial authority of the king entirely unrestricted except by his own act. Dionysius, however, answers elsewhere the query of Zumpt—If appeal were from the king to the assembly, who was to summon this assembly? The *deus ex machina* to solve this constitutional knot is the serviceable Brutus, created *Tribunus Celerum*, on account of his stupidity, by the last Tarquin[k].

---

a. Cic. de Rep. 1. 40. 62. tum prouocationes omnium rerum.

b. Dionysius 2. 12. βασιλεῖ...ἐξῄρητο (ὁ Ῥώμυλος) τάδε τὰ γέρα... παντὸς τοῦ κατὰ φύσιν ἢ κατὰ συνθήκας δικαίου προνοεῖν, τῶν τε ἀδικημάτων τὰ μέγιστα μὲν αὐτὸν δικάζειν τὰ δ' ἐλάττονα τοῖς βουλευταῖς ἐπιτρέπειν. Tullus takes counsel in the case of Mettius 3. 26.

c. Livy 1. 49. Cognitiones capitalium rerum sine consiliis per se solus exercebat. See too Dionysius 4. 42.

d. Criminal-recht Absch. 1. c. 9. p. 123. Mommsen (Hist. 1. 5. p. 72) takes much the same view.

e. De Rep. 1. 40. 63. noster populus in pace et domi imperat et ipsis magistratibus minatur, recusat, appellat, prouocat; in bello sic paret ut regi.

f. See the episode in Livy 8, 30—35.

g. Dig. 1. 2. 2. 16. qui (Consules) tamen ne per omnia regiam potestatem sibi uindicarent, lege lata factum est ut ab iis prouocatio esset, neue possent in caput ciuis Romani animaduertere iniussu populi.

h. Cic. de Rep. 2. 32. 56. Atque his ipsis temporibus dictator etiam est institutus decem fere annis post primos consules T. Lartius; nouomque id genus imperi uisum est et proximum similitudini regiae.

i. Livy 2. 18.

j. Dionysius 3. 22. ἀπορούμενος...κράτιστον εἶναι διέγνω τῷ δήμῳ τὴν διάγνωσιν ἐπιτρέπειν.

k. Dionysius Antiqq. 4. 71.

§ 15.

Right of Appeal imperfect.

On the whole the greater weight of tradition is undoubtedly in favour of the supreme and irresponsible character of the royal jurisdiction. This is also the view taken by most of the best modern authorities. It is that of Zumpt and that of Mommsen. Of the former, the fourth chapter of the first section of the Criminal-recht may be consulted with advantage. Mommsen places the kingly power almost higher than Zumpt. In a most interesting parallel drawn between the position of the king in the state and the *paterfamilias* in the household he says of the former, 'He had the same right as a father had to exercise discipline and jurisdiction.... He sat in judgment in all private and in all criminal processes, and decided absolutely regarding life and death as well as regarding freedom... When he had pronounced sentence of death he was entitled, but not obliged, to allow an appeal to the people for pardon[a].'

Now, that the offences first taken cognizance of by Roman judicature were derived from the idea of the family and punished by quasi-religious penalties connected with the same idea, I fully believe; but that the chief magistrate at Rome was ever entrusted with the full patriarchal power, is surely open to question; especially when we remember that the peculiar developement of the latter at Rome is considered with good ground[b] as a mere result of Quiritarian ownership, which could scarcely have been attributed to the king with respect to all the citizens. There are traces of sentence by the people in the old meaning of *sacer* (above § 6); of a meeting of burgesses for a quasi-judicial purpose in the *Contio* (§ 8); and the *lex* quoted by Livy as regulating procedure in *perduellio*, is in favour of appeal to the people as of course.

May we infer some right of a burgess, even though an imperfect right merely dependent on custom, to be tried upon certain charges by his peers? If so, the arrogation by a king of the power of adjudicating upon all cases without appeal, would justly be regarded as unconstitutional, and may have been one of the causes for the abolition of the regal power[c]. So that the lex Valeria, which had to be twice re-enacted, was possibly not so much the creation of a new constitutional right as the recognition and extension of an old one.

---

a. Mommsen Hist. 1. 5 (p. 67 of Dickson's translation).

b. Heineccius Elementa Iuris Civilis § 136.

c. It is only fair, however, to add that the very faint indications of what is regarded as arbitrary conduct of the king in passing capital sentences, have been explained as mere neglect to consult a *consilium*. Nor are all the offences stated as cases of *perduellio*. Dionysius makes it one instance of the ὠμότης attributed to Romulus that he ἐκέλευσεν ὦσαι κατὰ κρημνοῦ Ῥωμαίων τινὰς ἐπὶ λῃστείᾳ τῶν πλησιοχώρων κατηγορηθέντας...τὴν δίκην αὐτὸς μόνος δικάσας (Antiqq. 2. 56). The same author speaking of Tarquinius Superbus and his *delatores* (to put in word Dionysius' anachronism of fact) says (Antiqq. 4. 42) οἱ δ' ὑπάγοντες αὐτοὺς εἰς τὰς δίκας ἄλλους ἐπ' ἄλλαις ψευδέσιν αἰτίαις μάλιστα δ' ἐπιβουλεύειν αἰτιώμενοι τῷ βασιλεῖ κατηγόρουν ἐπ' αὐτῷ δικαστῇ. ὁ δὲ τῶν μὲν θάνατον κατεδίκασε τῶν δὲ φυγὴν κ.τ.λ. Superbus, says Livy (1. 49), cognitiones capitalium rerum sine consiliis per se solus exercebat.

See too Zumpt Criminal-recht Absch. 1. Cap. 9. p. 123. Mommsen Hist. 1. 5. p. 72 translation.

§ 16.

PERDUELLIO.

IT remains to consider what was the offence or class of offences for which this earliest recorded procedure was established.

Perduellio or *perduellis* was no doubt derived from *per* and *duellum* the old form of *bellum.* Flaccus evidently regards the prefix as being nothing but the preposition *per* in an intensitive sense*. It is more likely that we have here that "depreciative" or condemnatory *per* (Donaldson Varron. 10 § 7) which occurs in *periurus* and *perfidus,* and which certainly corresponds curiously in meaning with some uses of the Greek παρα- and the German rer- (Gothic *fair*). In this point of view comes naturally enough the meaning 'he who wars wrong,' or, 'on the wrong side,' i. e. *enemy,* which Flaccus tells us was the old meaning of *perduellio,* a statement borne out by the testimony of Gaius as to *perduellis* and the use of the latter word by Plautus and Ennius*.

As applied to a citizen, we should expect this word to mean, 'an enemy of his country,' and the concrete *perduellio,* that species of treason which *mutatis mutandis* answers to our 'levying war against our lord the king in his realm.' (25 Edward 3. c. 2). And this seems to be the idea, somewhat vaguely expressed, of Ulpian, when he tells us that not every man who is accused under the Lex Iulia Maiestatis, and dies while subject to the charge, forfeits his property, but only he who is accused of *per-duellio* as animated with a hostile mind against the commonwealth or emperor[e]. And those condemned for *perduellio* are coupled with hostes, as persons for whom mourning is not to be made[d].

Like our own 'treason' the word *perduellio* seems to have come to be taken in a conveniently extensive sense. This was the form of indictment probably brought against Sp. Cassius (A. V. C. 268), destroyed on the ground of attempting to make himself king[e]: against Gn. Fulvius for bad management and cowardice in military command (A. V. C. 541)[f]: against Ti. Gracchus and G. Claudius, for breach of the respect due to a tribune (A. V. C. 583)[g]: against G. Rabirius for the slaughter of the tribune Sa-turninus, thirty-seven years after the event; Saturninus being killed A. V. C. 654, and Rabirius defended by Cicero A. V. C. 691[h]. In later times, from the cases of Fulvius Gracchus and Claudius, it would appear that any violation of a high constitutional principle or any gross dereliction of duty in a public officer could be brought under this compendious form of accusation.

The coup d'état, too, in which Saturninus fell, might naturally be treated from its magnitude and tumultuous character as not an ordinary murder. But it is difficult to understand how the mere *parricidium* of Horatius could be considered as a state offence: nor can I see any reason for his being represented as charged with the latter crime, but the prevalent tradition that the accused of treason had that right of appeal, which is made available for the hero's escape. Nor is it impossible that in writing the words *clemente legis interprete*, which have not a very satisfactory sense if only applicable to the place where they stand, Livy may have had some thought of the merciful construction that treated a clear case of murder as a doubtful one of treason upon which the popular accused was sure to be acquitted. (See, however, as to these words § 13.) Zumpt, too, if I understand him rightly, takes this view of Tullus' conduct as described by Livy; with the exception of considering that there was previously no general enactment as to treason, and that Tullus' 'merciful interpretation' consisted in the issuing of a special mandate for this particular case, by which an appeal was allowed[1]. My objection to this last point has been stated above (§ 12) on the words *secundum legem.*

a.   Festus. *Duellum...*perduellio, qui pertinaciter retinet bellum.

b.   id.   *Hostis* apud antiquos peregrinus dicebatur et qui nunc hostis *perduellio.* See Corssen Beiträge p. 218 ed. 1863. Gaius in Digest 50. 16. 234. pr. quos nos *hostes* appellamus eos ueteres *perduelles* appellabant per eam adiectionem indicantes cum quibus bellum esset. Plautus Amphit. 1. 1. 97. Miles 2. 2. 69. Pseudolus 2. 1. 11. &c. Ennius ap. Varronem do L. L. 7. 49.

       The original meaning of *per-* was probably *otherwise* (i. e. than the right way). See Corssen Ausspr. 1³. 776. Compare too the Greek ἄλλως.

c.   Ulpian, Digest 48. 4. 11.

d.   Ulpian (quoting Neratius), Digest 3. 2. 11. 3. Non solent ... lugeri ... hostes uel perduellionis damnati.

e.   Livy 2. 41.

f.   Id. 26. 3.

g.   Id. 43. 16.

h.   Cicero pro Rabirio, argumentum.

i.   Criminal-recht Absch. 1. Cap. 7. p. 95.

§ 17.

THE QUAESTORES PARRICIDI.

THE question whether the *quaestores parricidi* were
ordinary officers or extraordinary commissioners, and
generally whether there was or was not in early times the
institution of police and public accuser, is of so much
interest that one is scarce free to avoid what must be
confessed to be a very difficult and unsatisfactory subject.
The name, of course, means investigators (trackers, *spürer*
is Mommsen's word). We may advert for one moment,
by way of illustration, to the modern word *detective*. They
were originally called quaestors, says Ulpian, quoting older
authorities, '*a genere quaerendi,* from that class (of their
duties) which consisted in investigation[a].' If these words
are to have another meaning, *i.e.,* 'from the *species* of
investigation which they conducted,' the first part of the
sentence should have run 'they were called *quaestores
parricidi* or *quaestores aerari,* according to the species,
&c.' The whole passage of Ulpian is appended[a]. So,
too, Varro derives the name from their duty of *searching
out* public moneys and crimes, which last, he says, 'are
now sought out (or investigated) by the *Tresuiri capitales*[b].'
This confusion of functions is the principal source of
difficulty throughout the subject.

First, as to the time when the office of *quaestor* came
into existence; all the authorities of Ulpian recognize
this office as established in regal times, not later than the
reign of Tullus. The opinion of ancient writers cited by
this jurist that Tullus first introduced quaestors into the
state, may be, but is not necessarily, a confusion of
quaestores with *duumuiri.* We have the authority of
Tacitus also that *quaestores* were instituted even during
the royal domination, which fact is shewn, he proceeds to

tell us, by a *lex curiata ab L. Bruto repetita*[c]. The quotation from Festus given above (§ 6, note c.) is in favour of high antiquity for *quaestores parricidi*, who may have been contemporaneous with the enactment containing the words *paricidas esto.* At least, the term *parricidium,* used in an improper sense, seems scarce likely to have been chosen for the distinctive appellation of an office, at a time very much later than the act of legislation by which that sense was given.

I proceed to consider the authorities which appear to make in favor of a *first* appointment of quaestors in republican times.

Livy places in the mouth of G. Canuleius (A.V.C. 309) an argument in favor of throwing open the consulship to the plebeians, drawn from the various changes and new offices which had already been introduced into the constitution. After enumerating the pontificate and augurate (here attributed to Numa), the census of Servius, the consulship, and the dictatorship, he proceeds: 'Tribunes of the plebs, Aediles, Quaestors there were none; it was ordained that they should be made. Decemvirs for drawing up laws we have within these ten years created and abolished from our state[d].' There is an unmistakeable order of time in the greater part of this passage. The *decemuiri* probably do not come into that order, because they are honored with special mention as holding an office which had not only been newly introduced but also, unlike the others, abolished. But Canuleius is clearly made to place the institution of the quaestorship at least after the time of the first secession. Nay, if the close coupling of the three last-named offices goes for anything, we should have expected the quaestors to be *plebeian* officers, or at least not exclusively in the patrician interest; yet down to A.V.C. 333 they were patricians[e].

Quaestores are first mentioned by Livy as indicting Sp. Cassius on a charge of *perduellio*, A.V.C. 269[f], where they are clearly official accusers and acting in the patrician interest. The same is the case with the quaestors who indict M. Volscius (A.V.C. 295, 6) for false witness[g]. The quaestorship in question is there shewn to be a *yearly* office.

Quaestores appear for the first time in Livy's history, as connected with the *treasury*, A.V.C. 308[h]. The Faliscan booty[i] is brought into their hands, A.V.C. 360, whereas in the year of Sp. Cassius' accusation, by *quaestores*, it is the consul who sells the booty and brings the proceeds into the public treasury[k]. These treasury *quaestores* would seem, however, to have been confined to home affairs until A.V.C. 333, when the proposal is made that beside the two city quaestors two should attend upon the consuls to assist them in war. The number is accordingly doubled, the office being thrown open at the same time to the plebeians[l].

Plutarch, in his life of Publicola, attributes to that worthy the institution of a treasury and two treasurers from the *younger* members of the community[l].

The testimony of Zonaras is only valuable so far as it may be regarded as practically that of Dio Cassius. His statement about the same Publicola is certainly of interest, if it can be depended upon, and is capable of the following interpretation, which appears to me the only one consistent with common sense. 'The management of the funds, too, he assigned away (from the chief officers, now consuls) to others, on which occasion the treasurers (ταμίαι) first began to exist, but were called by the name of quaestors, which (quaestors) first used to adjudicate on capital charges, whence, in fact, they have got this title, on account of their investigations and the search of the truth from these investigations; but afterwards they received the task of managing the common funds, and were called by the additional name of treasurers (? = *aerarii*). Subsequently the courts were entrusted to another body, and the former officers were only managers of the funds[m].'

Lastly, Pomponius, after mentioning the institution of the right of appeal from the consuls, and several other matters, not here material, proceeds: 'At the time of the secession of the plebs from the patricians, the former created tribunes for themselves, and also two officers from the plebs who were called Aediles. Subsequently, when the public treasury had begun to increase, that there might be officers to preside over it, quaestors were constituted to preside over the money, so called because created for the purpose of seeking out and preserving money. And because, as we have said, the consuls were not allowed by law to give sentence on the life of a Roman citizen without order of the people, therefore quaestors *used to be appointed* (constituebantur) by the people to preside over capital charges. These were called *quaestores parricidi*, and are moreover mentioned by the law of the Twelve Tables[n].'

The principal objection to a pre-republican appointment of *quaestors* lies evidently in the passage last quoted, for the appointment mentioned by Pomponius is clearly subsequent to the passing of the Valerian law *de provocatione*. The usual plan followed with this author has been, where expedient, to reject his testimony altogether, on account of the inaccuracies which it no doubt contains. Zumpt justly protests against such a proceeding, and gives a key to the explanation of Pomponius' statement in his very acute and scholarlike notice of the *tenses* employed by that author. *Constituebantur* must, he says, mean *occasional* not *periodic* appointment when regarded by the side of *constituti sunt* (Consuls and censors), *creauit sibi plebs* (tribunes), *constituerunt* (aediles), *constituti sunt* (quaestors of the treasury); but the masters of the knights, an occasional office, *iniungebantur dictatoribus*, and the perfect used of the dictators themselves is qualified by an *interdum*[o]. There is a slight weakness in the last point, and it might be said, too, that the perfects are all descriptions of the *first institution* of an office, while the two imperfects do not take that point of view; *iniungebantur* meaning 'used to be added' to the dictators already mentioned, *constituebantur* 'used to be appointed,' whether occasionally or periodically. Still the imperfect will undoubtedly bear Zumpt's interpretation, which is, I think, confirmed by the word *praeessent*, describing the functions of Pomponius' quaestors. There is no evidence of any weight shewing that the province of the older quaestors in criminal matters extended any further than the investigation of crimes, perhaps the apprehension of accused persons, and the promotion of charges; and *praeesse capitalibus rebus* would be a somewhat incorrect term to apply to such functions. On the other hand it is the exact term employed of the later occasional quaestors appointed to investigate and adjudicate upon particular criminal cases. Such was the appointment of the consuls to investigate the murder and sentence the murderers of Postumius, A. V. C. 341[p], of the dictator C. Maenius to investigate and try the cases of treason in Capua, and subsequently Rome A. V. C. 440[q]. It is worthy of remark that Livy in the latter case uses the coordinate form *quaesitor*, which (with *quaestio*) seems to have become appropriated to the criminal as distinguished from the fiscal business (*quaestura*). The former may have been the first appointment of an occasional quaestor with judicial powers; it is at least

significant that it comes so near the doubling of the
number of regular quaestors and the throwing open of
that office to the plebeians, A. V. C. 333'. But whether the
institution of occasional *quaestores* is to be placed between
333 and 341, or even earlier, I am convinced that we have
in them the second class of officers mentioned by Pomponius who were appointed occasionally by the people to
preside over capital charges, and who would very naturally
be confused with earlier *quaestores parricidi*, whom they
probably superseded.

For those yearly patrician quaestors who are so useful
in removing obnoxious plebeians do not appear in the
case of Sp. Maelius (A. V. C. 314), or at all, to my knowledge, after that of M. Volscius Fictor, A. V. C. 296. Here
comes in an important piece of evidence from Tacitus,
who tells us[e] 'that the power of selecting quaestors remained to the consuls until the people took upon themselves the appointment to that office as well as to others.
And there were created for the first time (*i. e.* of such
creation) Valerius Potitus, and Aemilius Mamercus in the
sixty-third year after the expulsion of the Tarquins (A. V. C.
307) to accompany the military operations. Subsequently,
business increasing, two were added to take charge at
Rome.' Valerius Potitus is doubtless the peacemaker of
A. V. C. 305, and the Valerius Poplicola Potitus successful in
the same year against the Aequi and Volsci; Aemilius
Mamercus possibly the military tribune of that name,
A. V. C. 316, victorious, as dictator, over the Veientes and
Fidenates next year. I mention these particulars as partly
in confirmation of Tacitus' statement that the quaestors
of 307 A. V. C. (the first quaestors, according to him,
elected by the people) were military officers, in which he
differs from Livy. But whether we suppose the fiscal or
military functions of these quaestors to have been prior,

in importance or time, the accounts of both Livy and
Tacitus are perfectly consistent with the idea of a great
change in the office of quaestor, A. V. C. 307. No longer
in the consul's nomination, it ceases to be the organ of
patrician impeachment, that is, the old *quaestores parricidi*, the right of nominating whom descended to the
consuls from the kings, here come to an end; it is of the
later regular quaestors, fiscal or military, that Canuleius
speaks two years later, whom, as elected by the people, he
treats as the only quaestors worth considering, and couples
with the tribunes and aediles.

The later quaestors mentioned by Pomponius have
been identified with a third class, the specially-appointed
judges no doubt referred to by Varro, as those *qui quaestionum iudicia exercerent*[b]: the earlier quaestors of Pomponius are fiscal authorities created subsequently to the
first secession[a]. Plutarch[l] and Zonaras[m] attribute the institution of officers of the treasury to Publicola; the latter
author, I think, implying that the officers to whom this
charge was given existed before, under the name of quaestors, derived from their function of investigating criminal
cases. Plutarch's statement that Publicola 'gave to the
people the power of appointing two of the young as treasurers' is highly improbable in itself, supported, as far as
I am aware, by no evidence, and directly contrary to the
assertion of Tacitus. Dionysius recognizes officers of the
treasury (ταμίαι) as existing at the end of the war with
Porsena[n]. He also speaks of Sp. Cassius' accusers as τὴν
ταμιευτικὴν ἐξουσίαν ἔχοντες[t]. While not setting great
store by the four last-mentioned authorities, I think they
may represent a fact:—that on or shortly after the abolition of royalty, some public funds were intrusted to the
care of the old *quaestores*[u]. This was natural enough if
the capital penalty in cases of which they had the in-

vestigation were occasionally commuted to a fine: and
their charge of this source of public revenue might
easily be extended to others. At the same time Livy's
silence is remarkable, and may indicate that the fiscal
functions of these officers were regarded as unimportant
compared with their criminal ones. Zumpt considers the
quaestorship of the treasury, introduced by Publicola, to
have been an *extraordinary* office until the fall of the
decemvirs. For this view, we must assume two pairs of
quaestors during the period in question; an assumption
surely unsupported by evidence*. But whatever may
have been the origin of the treasury quaestors, I hope
it has been sufficiently shewn that there is no insur-
mountable objection to the statements by Tacitus and
Ulpian of the existence of quaestors in the regal times,
nor to the identification of these with the patrician
accusers mentioned by Livy and with the *quaestores parricidi* of Festus—a distinctive title which could scarcely
have first originated with the appointment of the latter
occasional *quaesitores*. Neither is the discrepancy as to
the mode of election, between Tacitus and Ulpian, more
than apparent. According to the former the power of
selecting quaestors survived to the consuls from the kings
and the appointment was in some manner connected with
a *lex curiata*. According to the latter (or rather his
authority, Junius Gracchanus) Romulus and Numa had
each two quaestors whom they were in the habit of creating not by their own voice but by the vote of the
people. A more prevalent tradition, adds Ulpian, ascribes
the introduction of quaestors to Tullus, in whose reign
they certainly existed. I have not the slightest hesitation
in accepting the reconciliation of these two statements
given by Zumpt: that the quaestors were selected or
nominated by the kings, which nomination was afterwards

confirmed, and the royal nominees formerly *created* by a *lex curiata*, i. e. by the vote of the people, as Gracchanus says, assembled in the only assembly of those times, the *comitia curiata*. And this particular *lex curiata* becoming no doubt a common statutory form, was on the abolition of royalty repeated or revived by the consuls in the case of the *quaestores* whom they first nominated after the example of the kings. Perhaps the actual terms were preserved till later times, and bore express reference to kingly institution: perhaps it was the fact of this having been a *lex curiata*, backed of course by the tradition of revival by Brutus, which Tacitus regarded as proof that quaestors existed under the kings. Whether the early republican *quaestores parricidi* were, in their police functions, considered as endowed with a sort of *imperium* must be mere conjecture: but *leges curiatae* were principally employed, in the republican period, for conferring *imperium*.

This quaestorship was, as we have seen, in the republican times, annual: what it was in the regal times can only be inferred from the language of Tacitus and Ulpian. The expression used by the former 'quaestors were,' or 'the office of quaestor was instituted (perfect) even under the domination of the kings,' seems in favour of a standing office rather than an occasional commission. Ulpian's statement, that Romulus and Numa 'had two quaestors each whom they were in the habit of creating, &c.', also supports the idea of a standing office and, perhaps, periodic appointment.

The offences which came within the province of these officers were probably at first all murders of a free man uncondemned, but afterwards all matters of capital charge. Both these inferences may be fairly drawn from the words of Verrius Flaccus (above, § 6, note *c*). Nor could the

F 2

impeachment of Manlius and Volscius by the *quaestores parricidi* be otherwise explained, for neither of these was accused of any act of bloodshed. Thus every case of *perduellio* would be a proper one for the *quaestores* to prosecute, though of course every case of *parricidium* would not be one of *perduellio*. (See below, § 16.)

a. Dig. 1. 13. pr. § 1. Origo quaestoribus creandis antiquissima est et paene ante omnes magistratus. Gracchanus denique Iunius libro septimo de potestatibus etiam ipsum Romulum et Numam Pompilium binos quaestores habuisse quos ipsi non sua uoce sed populi suffragio crearent refert. sed sicuti dubium est an Romulo et Numa regnantibus quaestor fuerit ita Tullo Hostilio rege quaestores fuisse certum est. sane crebrior apud ueteres opinio est, Tullum Hostilium primum in rempublicam induxisse quaestores. et a genere quaerendi quaestores initio dictos et Iunius et Trebatius et Fenestella scribunt.

b. Varro de Ling. Lat. 5. 14. Quaestores a quaerendo qui conquirerent publicas pecunias et maleficia quae tresuiri capitales nunc conquirunt. ab his postea qui quaestionum iudicia exercerent quaestores dicti.

c. Tacitus Ann. 11. 22. Sed quaestores regibus etiam tum imperantibus instituti sunt: quod lex Curiata ostendit ab L. Bruto repetita. mansitque consulibus potestas deligendi donec eum quoque honorem populus mandaret. creatique primum Valerius Potitus et Aemilius Mamercus sexagesimo tertio anno post Tarquinios exactos ut rem militarem comitarentur. dein gliscentibus negotiis, duo additi qui Romae curarent. mox duplicatus numerus (A.V.C. 489). Florus Epit. Liv. 15 quaestorum numerus ampliatus est ut essent octo.

d. Livy 4. 4. At enim nemo post reges exactos de plebe consul fuit. quid postea?...pontifices, augures, Romulo regnante, nulli erant: ab Numa Pompilio creati sunt. census in ciuitate et descriptio centuriarum classiumque non erat: ab Ser. Tullio est facta. consules nunquam fuerant: regibus exactis creati sunt. dictatoris nec imperium nec nomen fuerat: apud patres esse coepit. tribuni plebis aediles quaestores nulli erant: institutum est ut fierent. decemuiros legibus scribendis intra decem hos annos et creauimus et e republica sustulimus.

e. Liv. 4. 43.

f. Liv. 2. 41. Sunt qui patrem auctorem eius supplici ferant: cum cognita domi causa uerberasse et necasse peculiumque filii Cereri consecrauisse; signum inde factum esse et inscriptum 'ex Cassii familia datum.' inuenio apud quosdam idque proprius fidem est a quaestoribus K. Fabio et L. Valerio diem dictam perduellionis damnatumque populo iudicio, dirutas publice aedes.

g. Liv. 3. 24. A. Cornelius et Q. Seruilius quaestores M. Volscio, quod falsus haud dubie testis in Kaesonem exstitisset, diem dixerant. 25. in quaestoribus *nouis* maior uis maior auctoritas erat. cum M. Valerio . . quaestor erat T. Quinctius Capitolinus qui ter consul fuerat. 29. Confestim se dictator abdicasset ni comitia M. Volsci falsi testis tenuissent: ea ne impedirent tribuni dictatoris obstitit metus. Volscius damnatus Samnium in exsilium abiit.

h. Liv. 3. 69. Signa eo ipso die a quaestoribus ex aerario prompta.

i. Liv. 5. 26.

k. Liv. 2. 42.

l. Plut. Publicola c. 12. ταμιεῖον ἀπέδειξε τὸν τοῦ Κρόνου ναὸν ᾧ μέχρι νῦν χρώμενοι διατελοῦσι ταμίας δὲ τῷ δήμῳ δύο τῶν νέων ἔδωκεν ἀποδεῖξαι.

Plutarch's date is towards the close of the first century of our era.

m. Zonaras 7. 13. καὶ τὴν τῶν χρημάτων διοίκησιν ἄλλοις ἀπένειμεν, ἵνα μὴ τούτων ἐγκρατεῖς ὄντες οἱ ὑπατεύοντες μεγὰ δυνῶνται· ὅτε πρῶτον οἱ ταμίαι ἤρξαντο γίνεσθαι κοαιστωρας δ' ἐκάλουν αὐτούς. οἱ πρῶτον μὲν τὰς θανασίμους δίκας ἐδίκαζον, ὅθεν καὶ τὴν προσηγορίαν ταύτην διὰ τὰς ἀνακρίσεις ἐσχήκασι καὶ τὴν τῆς ἀληθείας ἐκ τῶν ἀνακρίσεων ζήτησιν· ὕστερον δὲ καὶ τὴν τῶν κοινῶν χρημάτων διοίκησιν ἔλαχον καὶ ταμίαι προσωνομάσθησαν. μετὰ ταῦτα δ' ἑτέροις μὲν ἐπετράπη τὰ δικαστήρια ἐκεῖνοι δὲ τῶν χρημάτων ἦσαν διοικηταί.

Zonaras wrote the Χρονικόν, in his monastic retirement at Mount Athos, about the beginning of the twelfth century A.D.

n. Dig. 1. 2. 2. 16. Exactis regibus, consules constituti sunt duo... lege lata factum est ut ab iis prouocatio esset . . 20. iisdem temporibus cum plebs a patribus secessisset . . tribunos sibi . . creavit. 21. itemque . . duos ex plebe constituerunt qui etiam aediles appellati sunt. 22. deinde cum aerarium populi auctius esse coepisset, ut essent qui illi praeessent, constituti sunt quaestores qui pecuniae praeessent; dicti ab eo quod inquirendae et conseruandae pecuniae caussa creati erant. 23. et quia, ut diximus, de capite ciuis Romani iniussu populi non erat lege permissum consulibus ius dicere, propterea quaestores constituebantur a populo qui capitalibus rebus praeessent, hi appellabantur quaestores parricidi quorum etiam meminit lex duodecim tabularum.

A similar statement is attributed to Gaius by Lydus. 'Gaius' testimony would stand high at first hand: strained through this worthless medium it scarce deserves quotation.

Γάιος τοίνυν ὁ νομικὸς ἐν τῷ ἐπιγραφομένῳ παρ' αὐτοῦ ad legem xii Tabularum . . αὐτοῖς ῥήμασι πρὸς ἑρμηνείαν ταῦτα φησίν...

ἐπειδὴ δὲ περὶ κεφαλικῆς τιμωρίας οὐκ ἐξῆν τοῖς ἄρχουσι κατὰ Ῥωμαίου πολίτου ψηφίσασθαι προεβλήθησαν κυαίστωρες παῤῥικίδιοι (sic) ὡσανεὶ κριταὶ καὶ δικασταὶ τῶν πολίτας ἀνελόντων. De magistratibus 1. 26.

On this passage Fuss remarks, Forsitan et hic Lydus errauit ac Pomponi uerba (Digest. 1. 2. 2.) Gaio tribuit.

o. Criminal-recht Abtheil. 1. Anm. 41.

p. Livy 4. 51. Senatus consultum factum est ut de quaestione Postumianae caedis tribuni primo quoque tempore ad plebem ferret plebesque praeficeret quaestioni quem uellet. a plebe consensu populi consulibus negotium mandatur.

q. Liv. 9. 26. quaestiones decretae dictatoremque quaestionibus exercendis dici placuit...uersa Romam interpretando res: non nominatim qui Capuae sed in uniuersum qui usquam coissent coniurassentue aduersus rempublicam quaeri senatum iussisse...inde nobilitas (queri) ipsos .. dictatorem magistrumque equitum reos magis quam quaesitores idoneos eius criminis esse.

r. Livy 4. 43. in urbe . . moles discordiarum inter plebem ac patres exorta est coepta ab duplicando quaestorum numero, quam rem, praeter duos urbanos quaestores ut duo consulibus ad ministeria belli praesto essent, a consulibus relatam cum et patres summa ope approbassent, consulibus tribuni plebis certamen intulerunt ut pars quaestorum (nam ad id tempus patricii creati erant) ex plebe fieret.

The discord is allayed by the recommendation of the interrex L. Papirius Magillanus 'mediis copularent concordiam patres patiendo tribunos militum pro consulibus fieri, tribuni plebis non intercedendo quo minus quattuor quaestores promiscue de plebe ac patribus libero suffragio populi fierent.

s. Dion. Halic. Antiqq. 5. 34. ἐδήλωσε δ' ἡ πρᾶσις ἣν ἐποιήσαντο μετὰ τὴν ἀπαλλαγὴν τοῦ βασιλέως οἱ ταμίαι.

t. Dion. Halic. Antiqq. 8. 77. Καίσων Φάβιος . . καὶ Λεύκιος Οὐαλέριος Ποπλικόλας...τὴν ταμιευτικὴν ἔχοντες ἐξουσίαν καὶ διὰ τοῦτο ἐκκλησίαν συνάγειν ὄντες κύριοι...Σπόριον Κάσσιον . . εἰσήγγειλαν εἰς τὸν δῆμον.

Cicero, speaking of the same case, says *quaestor accusauit* (De Rep. 2. § 60). He retains the absurd story of the father's execution. One trusts that all the accounts of paternal brutality in this

family cannot be true. See, as to L. Manlius Imperiosus, Liv. 7.
4, as to T. Manlius L. F. Liv. 8. 6, 7, as to T. Manlius Torquatus
Liv. 54 Epit.

u. This is the view taken by Mommsen. (Book 2. ch. 1. p. 260 tr.)

v. Criminal-recht Absch. 1. cap. 5. pp. 54, 55. I may here acknow-
ledge the many valuable suggestions which I owe to this chapter:
inter alia as to the mode of reconciling the accounts given by
Tacitus and Ulpian of the election of the first quaestors.

§ 18.

EARLY CIVIL PROCEDURE. SACRAMENTUM.

WITH respect to the criminal law of regal Rome there is,
besides the few authorities hitherto cited, little or nothing
upon which any reliance can be placed. The king as
judge; sometimes availing himself of the aid of a 'counsel;' sometimes perhaps, in cases of minor importance,
delegating his judicial powers to individual 'judges'[a];
aided, in his quest of capital crimes, by the *quaestores parricidi;* appointing at his pleasure, in cases of treason, the
extraordinary *duumuiri;* allowing, though perhaps not
bound to do so, an appeal from the latter to the assembled burgesses—this is all that we can recognize with any
degree of confidence.

In civil law as distinguished from criminal—the former being understood to mean generally rules on the
violation of which proceedings can only be taken by the
private person aggrieved—we have no remnant of direct
legislation belonging to the regal period. In point of
procedure, tradition represents the king here again as
judge, deciding all those matters which in later times
came before private persons as *iudices* or *arbitri.* This
is certainly implied, if not expressly stated, in a compari-

son drawn by Cicero between early Greek and Roman kings[b]. Duties so engrossing are made by the same author the ground for an endowment of royalty with ample lands cultivated at public charge: but the power of delegating the judicial function is recognized, perhaps as an innovation, in the case of Servius administering justice by the alleged direction of Tarquinius Priscus[c]. The same delegation appears in the speech which Livy makes Tanaquil address to the people on the same occasion[d]; while the feigned case, whether turning upon contested property or a personal broil[e], in hearing which Tarquinius Priscus meets his death, is an instance of the comprehensive jurisdiction over the most minute affairs attributed to the kings.

So Dionysius tells us that in ancient times the kings settled the cases for the suitors by themselves, and their judgment was law[f]. But even Romulus (as we have seen above) only retains the decision on greater offences (which would seem to include private wrongs) himself, entrusting the lesser to the senators, doubtless as to individual delegates (τοῖς βουλευταῖς), not to the whole senate as a court (for which we should have read τῇ βουλῇ)[g]. The same king passes his decisions speedily on wrongs by citizen against citizen, deciding some himself, entrusting others to substitutes[h]. A delegated jurisdiction upon matters of contract seems to be assumed in the 'magistrates and courts' mentioned as existing under Numa: though the whole of this passage has most suspiciously the air of a moral theme[i]. Tarquinius Priscus hears the pretended case of the two hinds, which seems in this author to be a civil suit[e]. Finally Servius is presented to the people by Tanaquil, as appointed by the king to superintend 'all matters public and private'[k].

The oldest form of 'action' (see next section, p. 92)

known to us is not inconsistent with the view of royal jurisdiction here presented. And its reconciliation with that view is most satisfactorily effected by recognizing the close connection, if not the original identity, of the royal with the pontifical function. *Actio per sacramentum* is incorrectly apprehended as 'proceedings by legal *wager*,' because, of the two parties staking, while the one lost the other did not gain. *Sacramentum* was the solemn consecration of so many pounds of copper to public sacred purposes, each party to a suit depositing the whole amount, but only the loser's deposit being ultimately taken. From its proper meaning of the act or form of consecration the word passed to that of the sum deposited, in which sense it is explained by Varro and Festus. The decemvirs fixed the amount of deposit, by a rough *ad valorem* scale, in the coinage which Mommsen, probably with justice, supposes them to have introduced[l]. But there is no reason to suppose that they introduced the *actio per sacramentum* itself, which was doubtless the one form under which, in the very oldest times, all civil proceedings were brought[m].

The sum forfeited by the losing party must have served in some sort as a fee to the court for time and trouble expended: from which we may fairly infer that court to have been not unconnected with the *sacra*, to which that sum nominally went. The testimony of Varro on this point is interesting and significant. The plaintiff and defendant, says he, deposited the sum of money respectively *ad pontem*. Müller, who retains this reading, supposes it to mean some sacred place near that bridge which we have seen to be under the pontiffs' special care. But Augustinus' emendation, *ad pontificem*, for which *ad pontem* might very well be an abbreviation, seems to me infinitely preferable[n]. Either reading indicates a connection of the earliest jurisdiction over private suits with the pontificate. And whether we regard the king as a developement of the pontiff or no, it is certainly at least probable that this jurisdiction was, in the period represented by the first five reigns, confined to him *or some* other member of the sacred college. In respect of the latter, the view best reconciling the somewhat conflicting authorities appears to be that which regards it as originally consisting of four, with the king in the fifth place as *ex officio* chief, though not bearing the later title *pontifex maximus*[a].

a. See above, § 15, notes *b*, *e*.

b. Cicero de Republica 5. § 3. [Nihil esse tam] regale quam explanationem aequitatis in qua iuris erat interpretatio, quod ius priuati petere solebant a regibus: ob easque caussas agri...definiebantur qui essent regii qui colerenturque sine regum opera et labore ut eos nulla priuati negoti cura a populorum rebus abduceret. nec uero quisquam priuatus erat disceptator aut arbiter litis; sed omnia conficiebantur iudiciis regiis. et mihi quidem uidetur Numa noster maxime tenuisse hunc morem ueterum Graeciae regum.

c. De Rep. 2. § 38. quod, cum Tarquinius ex uolnere aeger fuisse et uiuere falso diceretur ille (Seruius) regio ornatu ius dixisset obaeratosque pecunia sua liberauisset, multaque comitate usus iussu Tarquini se ius dicere probauisset, &c.

d. Livy 1. 41. 'interim (Tarquinium) Ser. Tullio iubere populum dicto audientem esse. eum iura redditurum obiturumque alia regis munia esse,' &c.

e. Livy 1. 40. specie rixae. Dionysius Antiqq. 3. 73. βοῇ μεγάλῃ χρώμενοι τὴν παρὰ τοῦ βασιλέως βοήθειαν ἐκάλουν ἀμφότεροι παρόντων αὐτοῖς συχνῶν...συναγανακτούντων ἀμφοτέροις καὶ συμμαρτυρούντων· ὡς δὲ εἰσκαλέσας αὐτοὺς ὁ βασιλεὺς λέγειν ἐκέλευσε περὶ ὧν διεφέροντο, αἰγῶν μὲν ἕνεκα διαμφισβητεῖν ἐσκήπτοντο κ.τ.λ.

f. Dion. 10. 1. τὸ μὲν ἀρχαῖον οἱ βασιλεῖς ἐφ' αὑτῶν ἔταττον τοῖς δεομένοις τὰς δίκας καὶ τὸ δικαιωθὲν ὑπ' ἐκείνων τοῦτο νόμος ἦν.

g. Dion. 2. 14. βασιλεῖ...ἐξῄρητο τάδε τὰ γέρα...παντὸς τοῦ κατὰ φύσιν ἢ κατὰ συνθήκας δικαίου προνοεῖν τῶν τε ἀδικημάτων τὰ μέγιστα μὲν αὐτὸν δικάζειν τὰ δὲ ἐλάττονα τοῖς βουλευταῖς ἐπιτρέπειν προνοούμενον ἵνα μηδὲν γίνηται περὶ τὰς δίκας πλημμελές.

h. Dion. 2. 29. τῶν δ' εἰς ἀλλήλους ἀδικημάτων, οὐ χρονίους ἀλλὰ

ταχείας ἐποίει τὰς κρίσεις τὰ μὲν αὐτὸς διελὼν τὰ δ' ἄλλοις
ἐπιτρέπων.

i. Dion. 2. 75. αἵ τε ἀρχαὶ καὶ τὰ δικαστήρια τὰ πλεῖστα τῶν ἀμφισβη-
τημάτων τοῖς ἐκ τῆς πίστεως ὅρκοις διῆτων. ταῦτα...ὑπὸ τοῦ Νομᾶ
τότε ἐξευρεθέντα κοσμιωτέραν...τὴν Ῥωμαίων πολιτείαν ἀπειργάσατο.
It is not, however, clear whether he is speaking of the practice
in Numa's times or the subsequent results of Numa's ordinances.

k. τότε τὸν Τύλλιον (ἡ Τανακυλίς) αὐτοῖς συνίστησιν ὡς ὑπὸ τοῦ βασιλέως
ἐπίτροπον ἁπάντων τε τῶν κοινῶν καὶ τῶν ἰδίων ἀποδεικνύμενον.

l. Mommsen Hist. rei nummariae Rom. p. 175, quoted by Schöll. There
was still apparently only one denomination, the penalties of the
Twelve Tables being mere numbers, e.g. si iniuriam faxsit, xxv.
poenae sunto, see Schöll Reliqq. Praef. VIII, IX. As to the amount
of the penal sum, see Gaius Comm. 4. 14.

m. Gaius Comm. 4. 13. Sacramenti actio generalis erat &c. §§ 11
—32 contain almost all that we know of the actiones legis; a full
consideration of which belongs less to the present subject than to
that of the Twelve Tables. The *sacramentum* appears from
Festus to have been employed in criminal cases as well, by way
of a challenge from the accuser to the accused, in a certain sum.
Sacramentum aes significat quod poenae nomine penditur *siue eo
quis interrogatur* siue contenditur. This, however, belongs to the
most probably later jurisdiction of the *tresuiri capitales.* See
Epit. Liv. 11. In the part of Flaccus' article referring to the
latter (not here cited) *L. Papiri Tr. Pl.* is a contradiction in
terms. It is surprising that Müller does not see the necessity of
some such correction as that of Ursinus (*Tr. Mil.*) in spite of its
historical difficulties. Clodius would scarcely have been at the
trouble of a plebeian adoption if a Papirius could so long before
have been a tribune of the plebs. The triumuiratus nocturnus to
which a plebeian was eligible existed as early as A.U.C. 430. Liv.
9. 46.

n. De Lingua Latina 5. 180. Ea pecunia quae in iudicium uenit
in litibus *sacramentum* a sacro. qui petebat et qui inficiabatur de
aliis rebus utrique D aeris ad pontem deponebant, de aliis rebus
item certo alio legitimo numero assum; qui iudicio uicerat suom
sacramentum e sacro auferebat, uicti ad aerarium redibat.

o. See Cic. de Rep. 2. 14. 26. Livy 1. 20, 32 : 2, 2 : 10. 6. Dionysius
Antiqq. 2. 73 and Zumpt's excellent note, Criminal-recht, Erste
Abth. Anmerk. 61, p. 420. He suggests the original identity
between this board and the five officers who are mentioned by
Festus : the king, the three flamens, and the pontiff afterwards
maximus. It is very possible that the board was at first the

king, (maior pontiff proper,) the three flamens, and the minor
pontiff proper. See Macr. Sat. p. 15. 10.

§ 19.

EARLY CIVIL PROCEDURE. VINDICATIO. IN JURE CESSIO.

IT should never be forgotten that the English word *action*
scarcely conveys a correct notion of the Roman *legis actio.*
This might rather be rendered a *mode* or *stage* of statutory
civil proceedings. Moreover it could evidently not be the
first stage, but must have been preceded by claim on the
one part and counter-claim or denial on the other. The
'hand-grapple' (*manuum consertio*), that followed, was apparently symbolical of physical conflict, a meaning which
the phrase *manus conserere,* as applied to armies, retained[a].
Whether any such symbolism is to be found in the technical word expressing 'claim,' depends on a moot point of
etymology. Corssen connects the first syllable of the
words *uindex, uindicare,* &c. with a root signifying *desire*
(cf. Venus, &c.) ; so that *uindicare,* according to him, means
merely means 'to express desire[b].' Many, however, will
doubtless still prefer the old explanation of this word,
which Schöll accepts—that it means *uim monstrare,* 'to
declare or manifest force' in the case of a particular article,
whether this be the actual thing, the title to which is in
question, or a mere legal representative of it, *e.g.* the clod
from the estate[c]. Hereupon the question seems to arise
whether the force declared purports to be that of the
rightful owner, or of a deforciant. Mommsen (1. 11. p.
163, tr.) evidently considers the latter to be the case, but
although *uis* has this meaning in the Praetor's order, *quod
nec ui nec clam nec precario,* &c., I incline to the former in
uindicare, having regard to the phrase *uindicare in liber-*

tatem, and the fact that it is the claimant into liberty (to translate the phrase literally) who really does exercise the act of force by striking the person to be made free with the *uindicta*[d]. This word probably first meant the thing claimed, afterwards the claiming rod. So, in the *uindicatio in iure*, of which Gaius gives us such a graphic picture (4. 16), the claimant is in typical possession, not deforced from possession, of the slave on whom he lays the straw declaratory of his power. This is the *uis festucaria* of Gellius, 20. 10. 10. The subject of *uindiciae* belongs rather to the Twelve Tables from which the difficult expression *uindiciam ferre* is quoted by Ser. Sulpicius, according to Flaccus' article on *uindiciae*. Here it may suffice to say that from a comparison of this article with the passage in Gaius, it would appear as if *uindicia* at first meant claim; *uindiciae* the samples or parts brought into court emblematical of the thing itself in dispute; *then* intermediate possession *pendente lite*. The *partes* in Gaius are in most cases (for the *pilus* is doubtful) parts of the thing itself—as we should say in land, parts of the freehold—not of its produce. If they could be produce, this would explain the difficult phrase in Gaius 'litis et uindiciarum, id est rei et fructuum,' where, as the settlement of the *lis* relates to the thing, so the settlement of the *uindiciae* relates to its produce *pendente lite*[e].

This solemn form of claim, which must be made before the magistrate (*in iure*), was not employed solely as a preliminary to *sacramentum*. Various amicable transactions were placed on record, or legally validated, by the institution of collusive proceedings, which probably never went so far as the deposit.

Such was the *caussa liberalis,* whereby a slave who was to become a Roman citizen received manumission. This was without doubt a fictitious suit, in which the *uindex* or *assertor libertatis*, ultimately represented by the lictor, claimed the slave, not as his own property but 'for liberty' (*in libertatem*), and on the owner being silent or otherwise waiving *his* claim, the magistrate made award accordingly^d. Such, too, when an adoption was to be effected, was the surrender (*in iure cessio*) by which the *filius-familias* passed from his natural to his adopted father^f. And the two last-mentioned cases are probably only particular applications of a much more general principle—that of effecting alienation by a feigned suit, default on the part of the alienor, and award, by the magistrate, to the alienee. Of this species of assurance (*in iure cessio*) Gaius gives us an account in Comm. 2. 24. It was, according to Ulpian, a common form for the alienation of any thing whatever^g: and, according to Gaius, the *only* form by which certain incorporeal things, *e.g.* inheritances, usufructs, and servitudes of estates in Rome, could be assured^h.

No date can be given for the origin of this mode of assurance, which may have sprung into existence at any time after the establishment of a court or magistrate at all. With some kinds of property the artifice of a fictitious suit was doubtless adopted in the interest of the purchaser, whose best security against future proceedings would be a record of the court in which such proceedings must be instituted : with others^h, an exceptional limitation of the ordinary rights of ownership, or an avoidance of family obligation was perhaps thought to require magisterial sanction. The resemblance of our Common Recovery to the Roman Surrender in Court has been frequently remarked. It is perhaps scarcely necessary to point out the difference between the latter and its English namesake in Copyhold, where there is no suit, real or fictitious, between vendor and purchaser, and the lands are surrendered not to the purchaser (at least directly) but to the lord.

a. This view of *conserere manus* seems favoured by Varro de Lingua Latina 5, 7. Sic conserere manum dicimur cum hoste; by the common use of the phrase to indicate hostile encounter ; and perhaps by the lines of Ennius quoted in Noctt. Att. 20. 10.

> Non ex iure manum consertum sed mage ferro
> rem repetunt regnumque petunt, uadunt solida ui.

Ortolan (§ 1863, n. 2) takes the *consertio* to have been merely the simultaneous seizure of the disputed property, by the two parties. In favour of his view must be reckoned the explanation of Aulus Gellius in the passage cited (cum adversario simul manu prendere), and an article in Festus: *sertorem* quidam putant dictum a prendendo quia cum cuipiam adserat manum, educendi eius gratia ex seruitute in libertatem, uocetur adsertor. The preposition, however, in adscrere might well indicate taking to oneself by *sertio* (or *consertio*) similarly to the *ad* in *arrogare*. Gaius also (4. 16) only tells us of two simultaneous vindications, not of a symbolic contest.

b. Corssen Ausspr. 2^2. 272. Vindicare, if connected with *uis*, is a 'spurious compound' (unlike *causidicus* &c., which contain no case-suffix), unless we can suppose the Latins to have possessed at some time, besides their surviving stem *uis-* shewn in uires (for older *uises*), another stem in *n* corresponding to the Greek Ϝιν- in Ἰνες, ἰνίον, &c. See however Curtius Grundzüge, p. 362.

c. Aulus Gellius 20. 10. 9. et in ea gleba tanquam in toto agro uindicarent.

d. See Gaius Comm. 1. 17. Boethius in Ciceronis Topica, 2. § 10. Vindicta est uirgula quaedam quam lictor manumittendi serui capiti imponens eundem seruom in libertatem uindicabat dicens quaedam uerba sollemnia. See Ortolan's note on Iustin. Instt. 1. 5. 1, especially n. 4 to § 58 of the Explication.

e. Gaius Comm. 4. 16, 17. Festus *Vindiciae*. Not much is to be made out of the Pseudo-Asconius on Cicero Verr. 2. 1. § 115.

f. Noctes Atticae 5. 19. 1. Adoptantur autem cum a parente, in cuius potestate sunt, tertia mancipatione in iure ceduntur, atque ab eo qui adoptat, apud eum apud quem legis actio est uindicantur.

g. Ulp. 19. 9. In iure cessio communis alienatio est et mancipi rerum et nec mancipi quae fit per tres personas, in iure cedentis, uindicantis, addicentis.

h. Gaius Comm. 2. 29. 30. 34. Provincial estates were neither capable of mancipation nor of surrender (ib. 31), but of course these had no existence till long after the Regal period. Estates in Italy were capable of both (*ib.*).

§ 20.

THE SERVIAN REFORM. CRIMINAL AND CIVIL LAW.

HITHERTO the statements of historians have been considered rather as illustrative of ancient practice than as narrative of actual facts. It is not necessary, as has been before remarked, to discuss the question whether the time-honoured heroes of Roman legend ever existed or not. It is quite possible to believe in the early introduction of appeal without dating it by the reign of Tullus: nor do the *quaestores parricidi* require the names of Romulus or Numa to back them.

In reading of Servius, however, fabulous as great part of his story is, we find so much of the reform known under his name proved to be historical by its long surviving remains, that it seems scarcely wise at once to discredit even what Dionysius tells us further of the Commons' King, provided there be nothing improbable in the tale. And those who will not go so far as to believe in a personal Servius may yet perhaps consent to connect certain changes attributed to him with the occasion of the Servian reform, which is a fact beyond question.

There is no reason for thinking that any material alteration was made in criminal law : the appeals, if there were appeals, may have been to the new assembly of the centuries instead of the old one of the curies; but of this we have no proof*. A special penal enactment, directed against default in making return of the amount of the offender's property, is attributed to Servius both by Livy and Dionysius, the latter asserting that this law remained for a long time amongst the Romans. Livy rather treats the law as temporary, and it need not detain us here either on the score of importance or credibility[b].

The antiquity of the fragment against the striker of a parent, preserved by Festus (above § 6, note c), is probable on internal evidence. There is no necessity to press its reference to Servius, a reason for which may perhaps be found in his own tragical end[c].

While, however, no new criminal enactment of importance can be referred to this epoch, other branches of law in all probability sustained material alteration. The traditional popular character of Servius is scarcely accounted for by the constitution attributed to him, which, at least directly, assigned to the non-burgesses duties alone and not rights[d]. Accordingly we find, in the stories which reached Dionysius, besides the constitution (treated by that historian as a mere equitable assessment), most of the measures actually passed by later champions of the people, typified or exemplified in the person of the first. Servius puts taxation on a fair footing for the poor[e], pays the debts of their country's defenders out of his own pocket[f], and engages to forbid the pledging of personal liberty for the future[g]. Servius redistributes the public lands[h], and moreover gives homesteads to the 'hearthless' Romans around his own on the best part of the Esquiline[i]. All this bears, as has been intimated, a suspicious resemblance to the popular measures of the early republican period; and history, as we know she often repeats, may perhaps be said sometimes to anticipate herself. Besides these acts, however, of the first reformer, there are others not so clearly modelled upon those of his successors. He collects the laws of earlier kings, creating certain new ones himself: he has the laws relating to *contracts*, as well as to offences, ratified by the comitia curiata[j]: lastly, he diminishes the royal power by separating private from public charges, retaining cognizance of the latter himself, while he entrusts the former to private judges, whose powers and rules of procedure he settles by law[k]. A probable commentary on the last measure is furnished in the account given of the sufferings of the people under the next king. 'The laws enacted by Tullius, according to which they used to get their due from one another on terms of equality, and were in no wise subject to injury by the patricians, as before, in respect of their contracts—all these laws Superbus abrogated[l].' They are represented as being re-enacted, or at least recalled into use by the first consuls[m].

The changes which will now be noticed as probably connected with the Servian reform are in the law of civil procedure, of conveyance and contract, and of the family.

---

a. Mommsen insists upon the purely military character of the system of centuries at first. Its application to political purposes must, he thinks, be pronounced a later innovation. (Hist. 1. ch. 6. p. 100 of tr.). Incidentally, however, he allows that certain changes must necessarily have followed, for instance that it was the *centuries*, now, who interposed their authority to the testaments of soldiers made before battle (ib.). See below, § 23.

  A valuable and interesting disquisition on the *comitia centuriata* and their connection (or original non-connection) with the local *tribes* will be found in Mr Seeley's Livy, Book 1. pp. 76. 87.

b. Liv. 1. 44. Censu perfecto quem (Servius) maturaverat metu legis de incensis latae cum uinculorum minis mortisque edixit &c. Dion. Antiqq. 4. 15. τῷ δὲ μὴ τιμησαμένῳ τιμωρίαν ὥρισε τῆς τε οὐσίας στέρεσθαι καὶ αὐτὸν μαστιγωθέντα πραθῆναι· καὶ μέχρι πολλοῦ διέμεινε παρὰ Ῥωμαίοις οὗτος ὁ νόμος.

c. Liv. 1. 48.   Dion. Antiqq. 4. 39.

d. Mommsen Hist. 1. ch. 6. p. 95 tr.

e. Dionysius Antiqq. 4. 9. ἵνα...τὰς...εἰσφορὰς δι' ἃς οἱ πένητες ἐπιβαροῦνταί τε καὶ ἀναγκάζονται δανείσματα ποιεῖν κουφοτέρως εἰς τὸ λοιπὸν φέρητε, τιμήσασθαι τὰς οὐσίας ἅπαντας κελεύσω κ.τ.λ.

f. Dion. Antiqq. 4. 9. ἐκ τῶν ἐμαυτοῦ χρημάτων δίδωμι διαλύσασθαι τὰ χρέα. 10. πάντων ὁρώντων ἀπηρίθμει τοῖς δανεισταῖς τὰ χρέα.

g. Dion. Antiqq. 4. 9. νόμον θήσομαι μηδένα δανείζειν ἐπὶ σώμασιν ἐλευθέροις ἱκανὸν ἡγούμενος τοῖς δανεισταῖς τὰς οὐσίας τῶν συμβαλλόντων κρατεῖν.

h. Dion. Antiqq. 4. 10. ἐξέθηκεν ἐν φανερῷ διάταγμα βασιλικὸν ἐκχωρεῖν τῆς δημοσίας γῆς τοὺς καρπουμένους τε καὶ ἰδίᾳ κατέχοντας ἐν ὡρισμένῳ τινὶ χρόνῳ καὶ τοὺς οὐδένα κλῆρον ἔχοντας τῶν πολιτῶν πρὸς ἑαυτὸν ἀπογράφεσθαι.

i. Dion. Antiqq. 4. 13. διένειμε τὴν δημοσίαν χώραν τοῖς θητεύουσι. Ῥωμαίων...καὶ διένειμεν αὐτοὺς (τοὺς δύο λόφους) τοῖς ἀνεστίοις Ῥωμαίων οἰκίας κατασκευάσασθαι ἔνθα καὶ αὐτὸς ἐποιήσατο τὴν οἴκησιν ἐν τῷ κρατίστῳ τῆς Ἰσκυλίας τόπῳ.

j. Dion. Antiqq. 4. 10. νόμους τε συνέγραφεν ἐκ τῶν ἀρχαίων καὶ παρημελημένων ἀνανεουμένους οὓς Ῥωμύλος τε εἰσηγήσατο καὶ Νομᾶς Πομπίλιος οὓς δὲ αὐτὸς καθιστάμενος. 13. τοὺς νόμους τούς τε συναλλακτικοὺς καὶ τοὺς περὶ τῶν ἀδικημάτων ἐπεκύρωσε ταῖς φράτραις.

k. Dion. Antiqq. 4. 25. τὴν βασιλικὴν ἀρχὴν ἐμείωσε τὴν ἡμίσειαν τῆς ἐξουσίας αὐτὸς ἀφελόμενος· τῶν γὰρ πρὸ αὐτοῦ βασιλέων ἁπάσας ἀξιούντων ἐφ' ἑαυτοὺς ἄγειν τὰς δίκας καὶ πάντα τὰ ἐγκλήματα τά τε ἴδια καὶ τὰ κοινὰ πρὸς τὸν ἑαυτῶν τρόπον δικαζόντων, ἐκεῖνος διελὼν ἀπὸ τῶν ἰδιωτικῶν τὰ δημόσια, τῶν μὲν εἰς τὸ κοινὸν φερόντων ἀδικημάτων αὐτὸς ἐποιεῖτο τὰς διαγνώσεις τῶν δὲ ἰδιωτικῶν ἰδιώτας ἔταξεν εἶναι δικαστάς, ὅρους αὐτοῖς καὶ κανόνας τάξας οὓς αὐτὸς ἔγραψε νόμους.

l. Dion. Antiqq. 4. 43. τοὺς...νόμους τοὺς ὑπὸ Τυλλίου γραφέντας καθ' οὓς ἐξ ἴσου τὰ δίκαια παρ' ἀλλήλων ἐλάμβανον καὶ μηδὲν ὑπὸ τῶν πατρικίων ὡς πρότερον ἐβλάπτοντο περὶ τὰ ξυμβόλαια, πάντας ἀνεῖλε.

m. Dion. Antiqq. 5. 2.

§ 21.

IUDICES. LEGIS ACTIONES. CENTUMVIRI.

EXCEPT in the most patriarchal times, it is evident that such religious sanctions as that mentioned in § 9, must soon cease to suffice even a small community. In questions of the title to and the assurance of property as well as in matters of civil injury, a sort of 'common law' will grow up, of which cognizance must be taken sooner or later by the state tribunals if not by the legislature. The business that thus arose could not but very soon surpass the powers of any single man. So that even supposing criminal jurisdiction to have been confined to the more atrocious cases, and so capable of being discharged by the king or perhaps his occasional delegates, it could scarcely be so with civil business. Thus we should *à priori* arrive at the institution of some other court beside the king's, without the testimony of Dionysius, as a simple matter of necessity; and, if Cicero's statement to the contrary[*] be taken as anything more than an opinion that the traditional Numa came nearest to certain traditional Greek sovereigns, we can only say that the state of things which he describes could not long be possible. The best modern authorities admit the existence of *iudices* under the kings, whether their institution is to be attributed to Servius or not[b].

In the first days, however, of the *actio per sacramentum* as the sole form of civil proceedings, it seems not unlikely that this jurisdiction was confined to the king, and the other pontiff or pontiffs. The majority of cases would in all probability come before the latter, who were patricians and held their office for life. It is not likely that the most even-handed justice would be administered, by such judges, in cases where plebeians were concerned, especially if one party happened to be a plebeian and the other a patrician (see § 20, note l). We shall not be surprised, then, to find almost any change of jurisdiction from the pontiffs to a body of private judges (though the latter were mere delegates appointed at the magistrate's option) looked on as a popular measure. At the same time the permanent establishment of such a body might well be regarded as a certain narrowing of the regal power, which view Dionysius takes in a passage above quoted (20, note k), and in a speech of Servius. '*All* the power which ye gave me, I chose not to keep, but having established laws on the most important matters, which ye all ratified, I granted you the right of giving and receiving what is due, in accordance with these laws, and I myself first of all submitted to the rules of justice which I defined for others, obeying them like a private man[c].' The untranslatable Greek idiom διδόναι καὶ λαμβάνειν τὰ δίκαια, of course points exclusively to civil actions: and the tradition followed by Dionysius appears to have been that Servius enacted not only the severance of such cases from the ordinary royal jurisdiction, but also certain rules, both of principle and procedure, for the settlement of them, which were binding upon the whole community, the king included. Something like this view must have been taken by Tacitus, who tells us with his usual difficult brevity that Servius was the chief enactor of laws, laws which even the kings were to obey[d]. Whether the consent of the parties entered into the selection of the *iudex* we cannot say, but it seems that it did, and we know that such was the case with the *iudex* of the republican period. The language of Dionysius (§ 20, *n.* 1) is vague and coloured by his desire to represent the Servian administration throughout as a plebeian movement; for it cannot be true that plebeians were regularly or to any extent appointed *iudices*. There is no ground for contesting the universally received opinion that the *iudex* was, in the earliest times, always a senator. And admission of plebeians to the Senate, though perhaps possible before and somewhat facilitated by the reformed constitution[e], must have been very uncommon. Still it might be a great advantage for the plebeian to exchange the irremoveable pontiff, bound to no rule and amenable to no authority, for the *iudex* temporarily appointed, with powers and procedure defined, perhaps too selected by agreement of both parties or, if they could not agree, by lot. This is the grain of truth which I conceive to lie hid in Dionysius' chaff-heap : to go any further would be to anticipate the times of Gaius Gracchus[f].

From this Servian reform, then, probably date the civil proceedings 'by application for a judge' (*per iudicis postulationem*), in the account of which we are unfortunately deserted by our only safe guide. That part of the MS of Gaius which doubtless would have explained the *iudicis postulatio*, as well as the original *condictio*, is lost, unless we may place under the former head a scanty fragment (§ 15), which is generally connected with *sacramentum*. If we are to conclude, from this and the following section, that the appointment of a judge formed a necessary part or rather an inseparable accompaniment of *actio per sacramentum*, this too perhaps dates from the Servian reform. It may, however, not impossibly have been older, and taken place originally *in iure*, before the magistrate, whether king or pontiff, alone ; the application for a judge (*iudicis postulatio*) being the later means of importing a certain latitude into the rigid issues of the old law[g]. The original *condictio* was the mutual notice to attend, for the purpose of receiving the judge, given by the parties to one another[h]. Throughout the whole subject of the *legis actiones*, it must be remembered that they were not *actions* in our sense of the word, but statutory *forms* or *stages of procedure*, several of which may have entered into the same *action*, as we apprehend it.

Of the two remaining *legis actiones*, the *manus iniectio* which in the illustration given by Gaius approximates to our taking the person in execution, in all probability existed as a matter of what we should call common law before it was enacted by the Twelve Tables[i]. The *pignoris capio* of common law or custom (*moribus* Gaius 4. 26), if connected in the first instance with military pay, cannot have come into existence before that was introduced, according to Livy, A. U. C. 348[j]. The subject, however, of the *legis actiones* generally belongs to the law of the Twelve Tables, from which it is probable that the first four received both their statutory enactment and their name. For *in iure cessio* see above (§ 19).

The *iudices* of Servius Tullius have been often identified with the *centumuiri*, though the passage of Dionysius (4. 25) cited by Walter[k] in support of this view contains no allusion to the latter court. We do not know the date of its institution, but the *spear*, as the sign of Quiritarian ownership, is evidence of considerable antiquity[l]. We do know that the *centumuiri* dealt with many questions arising out of the ancient law of persons and things[m], and that the *actio per sacramentum* was retained as a preliminary to proceedings before them when elsewhere (except in one case) disused[n].

If the original constitution of this court is to be connected, as Verrius Flaccus and Varro intimate[o], with the thirty-*five* tribes, the *centumuiri* cannot have existed before A. V. C. 513, when that number (35) was made up[p]. The antique forms just referred to are against this, and the supposition that the name of *hundred* was given to a court which at its origin consisted of a hundred and five (perhaps exclusive of presidents) seems to me unwarrantable. The somewhat vague testimony of Pomponius on the subject[q], only amounts to a statement that, after the institution of a Praetor peregrinus (A. V. C. 512), *decemuiri litibus iudicandis* were made presidents of the *centumuiri*, which we know they continued to be till the time of Pliny the younger[r]. In a passage of Livy (3. 55) which treats of the re-institution of the tribunate of the plebs after the decemvirate, he couples with the tribunes and aediles *iudices* and

decemuiri who are clearly plebeian, and possibly as old in
point of institution as the tribunes themselves. The last-
named officers, though first erected into a magistracy on the
secession to Mons Sacer, may certainly have existed before
the secession, in connection with the local tribes, attributed
by consistent tradition to Servius. The original number of
these is so uncertain that little or no inference, as to the
centumuiri, can be safely drawn from it. Dionysius, in his
account of the Servian reform, gives authorities for thirty
and thirty-one*. The same author, when describing the
trial of Coriolanus, recognizes only twenty-one tribes to
which the vote was allowed, though his calculation that
the accused must have been acquitted 'for equality of
votes,' if he had gained those of two tribes more than he
did, assumes a total number of twenty-two*.

Livy represents the number of tribes as *made up* to
twenty-one in the year of Superbus' death (A.V.C. 259),
accounting for the other fourteen at different subsequent
periods". If the addition in A.V.C. 259 was of one tribe,
as has been supposed, the number originally established by
Servius may have been twenty, which suits very well with
that of a hundred officers.

The learned bishop of Lerida, Antonius Augustinus,
appears to have considered the *centumuiri* and their presidents as plebeian petty magistrates. I have not been able
to find Augustinus' treatise *De Legibus*, knowing him only
by his excellent account of Roman families. For the
above quotation of his opinion on the present subject I
rely upon Drakenborch's note to Livy, 3. 55. Both Drakenborch and Augustinus recognize a *lex Aebutia de centum-
uiris*—in all probability the same as that by which the
old *legis actiones* were abolished except in cases *damni
infecti* and those which were to come before the centumviral court. The date of the *lex Aebutia* is matter of great

question, though the institution of a Praetor Peregrinus
(A. v. c. 512), and the entire remodelling of civil procedure
which evidently then took place, seem to me quite as
likely an epoch for this law's enactment, as that usually
given (circiter 573). It may have been part of this remodelling to set aside the centumviral court for questions
of pure Quiritarian ownership where the old forms of procedure would most naturally be retained[v]. But the origin
of the court must, I think, clearly be placed very much
earlier—probably in Servian times. The expressions of
Dionysius quoted above, though they have a certain meaning when applied to the appointment of patrician (or at
least senatorial) *iudices*, have a much better one when
applied to the co-ordinate institution of plebeian *centumuiri*
for the hearing of plebeian cases. This, of course, ceased to
be the characteristic of the court in later times, when we
find it dealing with questions of *status*, inheritance,
testament, and Quiritarian law generally, irrespective of
order[w].

---

a. See § 18. note b.

b. Walter (trad. par Laboulaye), Procédure civile chez les Romains,
ch. 1. Ortolan, Histoire de la législation Romaine, §§ 162. 117.
Zumpt, Criminalrecht. Absch. 1. c. 4.

c. Dion. Antiqq. 4. 36. καὶ τὴν ἐξουσίαν ἣν ὑμεῖς ἐδώκατέ μοι...οὐχ
ἅπασαν ἐβουλόμην ἔχειν ἀλλὰ νόμους τε ὑπὲρ τῶν κυριωτάτων καταστη-
σάμενος οὓς ἅπαντες ἐπεκυρώσατε κατὰ τούτους ὑμῖν ἀπέδωκα διδόναι
τὰ δίκαια καὶ λαμβάνειν, καὶ αὐτὸς ἐξηταζόμην πρῶτος οἷς ὥρισα κατὰ
τῶν ἄλλων δικαίοις ὥσπερ ἰδιώτης πειθόμενος.

d. Tacitus Ann. 3. 26. sed praecipuos Seruius Tullius sanctor legum
fuit quis etiam reges obtemperarent.

e. Mommsen Hist. 1. 5. p. 70 tr. and 1. 6. p. 100 tr.

f. Zumpt (Absch. 1. cap. 4.) considers that Servius was the institutor
of iudices, who were senators individually appointed for each case
according to the agreement of the parties. For later changes in
the constitution of the judicial body see the laws Sempronia,
Liuia, Plautia, Cornelia, Aurelia.

g. Ortolan (§§ 1870, 1875) considers the procedure by *iudicis postulatio* to have gradually encroached upon that by *sacramentum*, from which it was of course distinct, as appears by Gaius Comm. 4. 20. He treats the judge, however, as necessarily entering into the sacramental procedure also (§§ 1861, 1900), relying principally, as it seems, upon a note of the pseudo-Asconius to Cicero's first count of accusation against Verres. (In Verrem 2. 1. c. 9 § 26.)

Namque cum in rem aliquam agerent litigatores et poena se sacramenti peterent poscebant iudicem qui dabatur post trigesimum diem.

This no doubt tallies with the *number* xxx in Gaius 4. 15, before which there is a hopeless lacuna. As far as **Gaius** alone is concerned the point turns upon whether we are to supply in the following sentence [idque] per legem Pinariam factum est; ante eam autem legem . . . . dabatur iudex the word *confestim* or *statim*, with Buttmann and Hollweg, or (as I should prefer) the word *nondum* with Heffter.

I question whether much independent value should be attached to the general statement of the pseudo-Asconius. If the following note about the personal examination of witnesses come from his hand, he cannot, according to Baiter, have written before the time of Hadrian, who established the stricter treatment of evidence. Analecta ad pseudo-Asconium. Onomasticon. See too Digest. 22. 5. 3. 1. The assertion, therefore, that application was made for a judge where proceedings *in rem* were taken *per sacramentum* may very well be no independent testimony but merely derived from Gaius' own account of *two* stages of the law on that point.

h. See Gaius Comm. 4. 18 for the *condictio*. Condicere is inadequately rendered by *denuntiare:* it must have originally signified *mutual* notice or notice *about something* agreed upon, not notice simply, or the preposition is meaningless. An agreement between the two parties as to the *iudex* is indicated by the old formula which Festus has preserved us under *Procum* . . est enim procare poscere ut cum dicitur in iudice conlocando *si alium procas niue eum procas* hoc est poscis. We know, too, that *mutual* notice was given to appear before the judge, when appointed. See Gaius 4. 15, **who** is here perfectly consistent with the pseudo-Asconius (loc. **cit.**) comperendinatio est ab *utrisque litigatoribus inuicem sibi denuntiatio* in perendinum diem.

i. For *manus iniectio* see Gaius Comm. 4. 21—25. The term of course is applicable to any form of arrest. It was effected not by an officer but by a private person, see Liv. 2. 23: 3. 44. &c., and might apparently (from the last-cited passage and others) **take** place *extra ius* i.e. not before the magistrate. See, however, Gaius Comm. 4. 29.

j. Livy 4. 59. See Aulus Gellius 6. 10. Verba Catonis sunt...pignoriscapio ob aes militare quod aes a tribuno aerario miles accipere debebat, &c. When pay for service actually began is doubtful. The *word* stipendium cannot have existed before the introduction of coined money, if the derivation in Festus be correct. Stipem . . nummum signatum. Müller, pp. 296. 313. 'Stamped' or 'pressed' seems a correct expression to us, though it should be remembered that the old coins were not *stamped* but *struck* with a hammer and double die. I fail to see the slightest connection in meaning between Corssen's translation of *stips* (kleines Geldstück 1². 505) and that of the other words with which he justly connects this, (stipulus stipes stipare, στῖφος, στύπος, στυφελός, &c.). Surely the notion of close pressure is the connecting link?

If the allowance for purchase of a horse and that for forage (*aes equestre* and *aes hordearium*) are to be connected, as Livy (1. 43) connects these, with the Servian military system; *pignoris capio*, being the means provided for their recovery (Gaius 4. 27), must have had an earlier date than that given in the text. Cicero (de Republica 2. 20. 36) appears to confirm Livy's account of the early institution of these allowances, referring them, however, to Tarquinius Priscus, and connecting them with Corinth, the fabled home of the Tarquinii, so as to throw discredit upon the whole story.

k. Tr. Laboulaye Procédure Civile, ch. 1.

l. Gaius Comm. 4. 16. Valerius Maximus 7. 7. 2: 7. 8. 1, 4.

m. Cicero de Oratore 1. 38. 173.

n. Gaius Comm. 4. 31, 95.

o. Festus. Centumuiralia iudicia a c uiris sunt dicta. nam cum essent Romae xxxv tribus quae et curiae sunt dictae terni ex singulis tribubus sunt electi ad iudicandum qui c uiri appellati sunt: et licet quinque amplius quam centum fuerint, tamen quo facilius nominarentur c uiri sunt dicti. Varro de Re Rustica 2. 1. . . numerus non ad amussim ut cum dicimus mille naues ad Troiam isse, centumuirale iudicium Romae.

p. Florus Epit. Liv. 19.

q. Dig. 1. 2. 2. 28. . . creatus est et alius Praetor qui peregrinus appellatus est . . 29. deinde cum esset necessarius magistratus qui hastae praeesset decemuiri litibus iudicandis sunt constituti.

r. Epist. 5. 21. The presidency appears to have been towards the close of the republic usurped by the ex-quaestors but was restored to the decemuiri by Augustus. See Suetonius Augustus c. 36 and

Torrentius' note, who adduces, against the suggestion of a first institution of these officers by Augustus, the antique s (of STLIS) found in inscriptions (XVIR. SL. IVDIK.). The *decemuiri* were still presidents when Cicero was a young man (pro Caecina 33 § 97).

s Antiqq. 4. 15.

t. Antiqq. 7. 64. μιᾶς . . καὶ εἴκοσι τότε φυλῶν οὐσῶν αἷς ἡ ψῆφος ἀνεδόθη τὰς ἀπολυούσας ἔσχεν ὁ Μάρκιος ἐννέα· ὥστ' εἰ δύο προσῆλθον αὐτῷ φυλαὶ διὰ τὴν ἰσοψηφίαν ἀπελύετο ἂν ὥσπερ ὁ νόμος ἤξίου.

u. Livy 2. 21. Romae tribus una et uiginta *factae*. As to the others see 6. 5; 7. 15; 8. 17; 9. 20; 10. 9; and the epitome of book 19.

v. Gaius Comm. 4. 30. Gellius Noctes Atticae 16. 10.

w. See pro Caecina 33 § 97 cum Arretinae mulieris libertatem defenderem. also ib. 18 § 53. As to *inheritance*, here concerning *both* orders, Cic. de orat. 1. 39. Quid qua de re inter Marcellos et Claudios patricios cuiri indicarunt?...nonne in ea caussa...de toto stirpis ac gentilitatis iure dicendum? As to *testament* see Valerius Maximus 7. 7. 1, 2; 7. 8. 1, 4. Digest 5. 2. 13, 17. Generally Cic. de orat. 1. 38. § 173.

§ 22.

Mancipium, Nexum.

The intermixture of what we term *common* with statute law is of course unavoidable in the account of any early legislation. With the oldest enactments of Rome, as with those of our own country, it is often evidently the case that they are merely 'declaratory of the common law.' That is, there is first the custom, then the specific act of the legislature recognising, sanctioning, and regulating that custom*. Thus from the provisions of the Twelve Tables may be clearly inferred the previous existence of those very ancient assurances or acts in law, *nexum* and *mancipium*, of which some notice seems proper here. As the institution of *iudices* is directly connected by ancient tradition with Servius, so that of *mancipation* has been indirectly connected by modern inference with the Servian reform.

Mancipium, from *manus* and *capere*, is evidently an expression originally proper of the taker, not the giver. Later, doubtless, the secondary verb, *mancipare*, was used of the latter: but at first it is the taker who is considered as the acting party, and *purchase* rather than *conveyance* is the correct translation of *mancipium*. I need not remind the reader of English Law that, under the legal term *purchase*, the notion of paying a *price* is not necessarily included. A price certainly enters into the earliest form of *mancipium* which has come down to us, but the word signifies only a taking by hand. Mommsen, accepting this bare physical meaning, refers the first mancipium to a time before the invention of property in immoveables, considering it primarily applicable only to objects which are acquired by grasping with the hand— such as slaves and cattle[b]. Whether we are to remount or no to this hoar antiquity, we may, I think, assume that *manus*, in the phrase *manu capere*, carried with it that peculiar idea of power and possession which we know belonged to the same word with reference to a wife in much later times. This power and possession was asserted by the symbolical 'hand-seizure,' which, when accompanied by the formal words, the payment of the piece of copper to the seller or its acceptance by him, all before the proper witnesses, operates as the original Roman conveyance, which we may now for convenience call by the later term, *mancipation*[c]. Ortolan, comparing the use of the lance as the well-known symbol of Quiritarian ownership, justly, in my opinion, regards the earliest mancipium as an emblem of capture[d]. And the same view is shewn in a definition by Florentinus of the word *man-*

cipium, used, it is true, in the later sense of the thing
taken rather than the taking, but defined as that which
is taken by (force of) hand from the enemy[e]. It is highly
probable that the five witnesses required for this assurance were intended to represent the five classes of the
census. If so, *mancipation*, as we know it, would seem to
have been subsequent to the Servian reform, or perhaps
part of the new system thereby introduced[f]. Whether
this mode of conveyance was originally intended to be
confined to certain kinds of property, or that construction
was, as Mommsen holds, a misunderstanding of later
times, we need not here enquire. It was doubtless regarded from the earliest times as specially applicable to
the things which came to be known as *res mancipi* (objects of *mancipium*), and which are clearly the articles of
most value in an infant agricultural state. Of these
articles the law, apparently, did not at first recognize any
other mode of assurance than *mancipation:* whereas
other property, at least if corporeal, might legally pass by
mere delivery (*traditio*)[g]. The doctrine that enjoyment
(*usus*) for a certain time should enure to ripen imperfect
ownership arising from irregular alienation into that full
ownership recognized by the ancient law of the Quirites
(*dominium Quiritarium*), was probably one of the earliest
equitable modifications imported into that law by judicial
authority (see below, p. 141).

The exact force of the *nexum*, and its connection with
mancipium, are matters of some difficulty. The latter is
coupled with the former by the particle *que* in the Twelve
Tables, which fact would seem rather to make against the
opinion held by some, that *mancipium* is a mere species
of the genus *nexum*. This opinion is based on the definition of Manilius, preserved by Varro. '*Nexum* is any
transaction by balance and copper, under which head are

mancipia.' A much more valuable definition follows, by the great jurist Scaevola.

'Mucius makes *nexa* to be things which by copper and balance *become subject to obligation* besides those things which *are given* by *mancipium.*' 'That this is the truer view,' adds Varro, 'the word in question itself shews; for the very thing which by balance becomes subject to obligation and not its own, is thence called *nexum.* The free man who owed his labour for servitude, in consideration of certain money, until he should pay that money, is called *nexus,*' &c.[b] The difference between Manilius and Mucius appears to be that the former is speaking of *nexum,* the act in law, the latter of *nexum,* the thing or person affected by that act in law. But the statements of both are perfectly in harmony with the view that the primary idea of *nexum* is obligation, affixed by law to the receipt of a nominal consideration. Some parallel may be found in the *bargain and sale* of our common law, by which a *use* was raised on the payment of any, even the smallest, sum of money. (A use, too, we may remember, originated in the *obligation* on the conscience of the *terre-tenant.*) So *nexum,* obligation, most likely originated in an actual bargain and sale of future services; and, if we consider *mancipium* as a conveyance, it would probably be more correct to say that *nexum* arose out of *mancipium* than that *mancipium* was a species of *nexum.* The two original ideas of acquisition and obligation are so combined in the earliest form of *mancipium* known to either us or our authorities, that confusion between them was and is inevitable[i]: but, however complex the ancient legal conception or transaction was, I cannot believe that the proper and primary signification of *nexum* was anything but *bond* or *obligation.* And, generally, the things affected by such an assurance are those which 'become subject to obligation (*nexa*) by copper and balance,' as distinguished from those which 'are given (out and out) by mancipium' (see page 111). This is the well-known use of the word in Livy, and the persons who place themselves in this position are said *nexum inire*, to enter into a bond or obligation.

Verrius Flaccus gives the first definition of Varro, attributing it to Gallus Aelius, and adding, as instances of *nexum*, *testamenti factio*, and (if the emendations be correct), *nexi datio* and *nexi liberatio*[k]. The two latter are most probably the giving and releasing of the bond or engagement by which the poor debtor became liable to personal servitude, and, to quote the graphic language of Varro, 'not his own.' The *testamenti factio* is, of course, the third mode of will-making mentioned by Gaius[l], which will be more particularly noticed hereafter (§ 23).

The old transaction, then, out of which both *mancipation* and *nexum* grew, being a bargain and sale for value, where the article purchased is present property, absolutely transferred, the business would seem to be over, and the *nexum*, or bond between the parties, at an end; where anything is left to be done, i.e. where the article purchased includes, or is, some future service, the *nexum* continues. Herein lies the important truth, ably put by Mr Maine, that in the original popular, as well as in the professional view, a contract was regarded as an incomplete conveyance.

It is not impossible that, even where property was absolutely and *finally* transferred, there may still have been a *nexum* subsisting. It seems that conveyances in this legal form fixed on the seller special liability of making good his title as owner, or at any rate of guaranteeing the purchaser in possession[m]. So, in our own law, if before the statute of *quia emptores* a man enfeoffed another in fee by the feodal word *dedi*, the law annexed a warranty to this grant. Therefore, even when *mancipium* or *mancipatio* was an absolute sale and complete transfer of property, the seller might still remain, to a certain extent, *nexus*, though the more natural and intelligible application of the term is to such cases as those instanced by Flaccus, where the main part of the transaction consisted of stipulations between the two parties, which were yet to be fulfilled. A good example of this subsisting *nexum* occurs in the *mancipatio fiduciae caussa*, or conveyance on trust. This was employed in the ceremony of emancipation, and other modes of modifying the legal condition of persons[n]; as applied to *things*, it was probably the earliest form of a mortgage[o] and trust deed[p].

Whatever of a limitative or executory character accompanied any particular mancipation was doubtless originally set forth in the *lex* or *binding contract*[q] of the *mancipium*, which was first orally declared *nuncupata* (see next section, p. 119), but afterwards reduced to writing and corresponded to our modern limitations, uses, trusts, covenants for title, provisoes—in fact everything which follows the words of grant in a conveyance.

---

a. So we are told Frag. Vatic. § 50, et mancipationem et in iure cessionem lex duodecim tabularum confirmat.

b. Mommsen Hist. 1. 11. p. 162. n. tr.

c. On the legal form of *mancipium* the locus classicus is Gaius Comm. 1. 119.

d. Histoire §§ 88—90.

e. Dig. 1. 5. 4. 3. Mancipia dicta quod ab hostibus manu capiantur.

f. Ortolan Hist. loc. cit. Mommsen Hist. 1. 6, p. 100 tr.

Festus. *Classici* testes dicebantur qui signandis testamentis adhibebantur. These, we know, were identical with the witnesses to mancipation.

g. See Mommsen Hist. 1. 11, p. 162, n. of tr. Ulpian. Frag. 19. 1. Mancipi res sunt praedia in Italico solo, tam rustica qualis est fundus quam urbana qualis domus; item iura praediorum rus-

R. L.   H ticorum uelut uia iter actus aquaeductus; item serui et quadrupedes quae dorso colloue domantur uelut boues muli equi asini. ceterae res nec mancipi sunt.

Again id. 19. 3. **Mancipatio** propria species alienationis **est** rerum mancipi. Compare Gaius Comm. 2. 22.

h. Varro de lingua Latina 7. § 105. *Nexum* Manilius scribit omne quod per libram et aes geritur, in quo sint mancipia. Mucius quae per aes et libram fiant ut obligentur praeter quae **mancipio** dentur. hoc uerius esse ipsum uerbum ostendit de quo quaerit; nam idem quod obligatur per libram neque suum fit inde *nexum* dictum. liber qui suas operas in scruitutem pro pecunia quadam debebat dum solueret *nexus* uocatur. The personal construction *fiant ut obligentur* is peculiar and not quite to be explained by Lucretius' *impersonal* pleonasm *fit ut*....I do not see, however, how it can bear any other meaning than that given in the text. The difficulty very probably arises from the confusion between *nexum* the thing bound and *nexum* the bond, of which I think traces may be seen in the passages cited below (*k*) from Festus.

i. See Maine's Ancient Law, ch. ix. especially pp. 314—316.

k. Festus. *Nexum* est, ut ait Gallus Aelius quodcunque per aes et libram geritur, idque necti dicitur, quo in genere sunt haec: testamenti factio nexi *datio* nexi *liberatio.* (Müller for *dando* and *liberanto*. Again *nexu* aes apud antiquos dicebatur pecunia quae per nexum obligatur.

l. 'per aes et libram' Gaius Comm. 2. 102.

m. See Mommsen Hist. 1. 11, p. 162 tr. As *auctoritas* or warranty certainly accompanied those imperfect assurances, the title under which might be ripened by *usus* into Quiritarian ownership, we should à *fortiori* expect it to accompany *mancipation*. It seems questionable, however, whether this continued to be the case, in later times, with mancipations by a mortgagee for the nominal sum of one sesterce. See Poste's Gaius p. 532 and below, note *p.*

n. Gaius Comm. I. 114, 115. Iust. Instt. 3. 2. 8, also below, § 25.

o. Isidor. Origg. 5. 25. Fiducia est cum res aliqua sumendae mutuae pecuniae gratia uel mancipatur uel in iure ceditur.
Isidorus Hispalensis, so called from his bishopric of Seville, flourished at the beginning of the seventh century of our era. 'Anno 636,' says Bellarmine, 'migrauit in caelum, ut ex chronicis Hispaniensibus intelligitur.' His *Origines* or *Etymologiae* contain many derivations and explanations which have considerable antiquarian if not much philological value.

p. The two cases of mortgage and trust are distinguished by Gaius in Comm. 2. 59. qui rem alicui fiduciae caussa mancipio dederit

uel in iure cesserit, si &c., and 60 fiducia contrahitur aut cum
creditore pignoris iure aut cum amico quod tutius nostrae res
apud eum essent.

Compare, as to trust, Boethius on Cicero's Topica 10 § 45.
Fiduciam...accepit cuicunque res aliqua mancipatur ut eam manci-
panti remancipet ; uelut si quis tempus dubium timens amico
potentiori fundum mancipet ut ei, cum tempus quod suspectum
est praeterierit, reddat. haec mancipatio fiduciaria nominatur
idcirco quod restituendi fides interponitur.

A most interesting relic was discovered in the year 1867 near
the mouth of the Guadalquivir in the shape of a brazen tablet
having inscribed upon it a form of mortgage by mancipation, to
secure present and future advances, with a power of sale.   The
estate mortgaged is conveyed to the mortgagee *uti optumus max-
umusque esset*, which according to Digest, 21. 2. 75 means that it
is to be guaranteed liber ab omni seruitute to the mortgagee.   He,
on the other hand, in case of sale, is not bound to make more
than a formal mancipation for a single sesterce, which apparently
did not involve warranty of title (Poste's Gaius, p. 532).   Hübner
attributes this tablet, from the form of the letters, to the first
century A.D.   I give the *lex mancipi* in full from Bruns' Fontes
Iuris Romani pp. 131, 2.   It is also to be found in the addenda to
Poste's edition of Gaius.

Dama L. Titi ser(uos) fundum Baianum, qui est in agro, qui
Veneriensis uocatur, pago Olbensi, uti optumus maxumus-q(ue)
esset HS n(ummo) I et hominem Midam HS n(ummo) I fidi fiduciae causa mancipio accepit ab L. Baianio, libripende autest(ato).
adfines fundo dixit L. Baianius L. Titium et C. Scium et populum
et si quos dicere oportet.

Pactum comuentum factum est inter Damam, L. Titi ser(uom)
et L. Baian(ium) : quam pecuniam L. (Titius L.) Baianio dedit
dederit, credidit, crediderit, expensumue tulit tulerit, siue quid
pro eo promisit promiserit, spopondit (*spoponderit*,) fideue quid
sua esse iussit iusserit, usque eo is fundus eaque mancipia fiducia
(e) essent, donec ea omnis pecunia fidesue persoluta L. Titi
soluta liberataque esset ; si pecunia sua quaque die L. Titio
h(eredi)ue eius data soluta non esset, tum uti eum fundum eaque
mancipia, siue quae mancipia ex is uellet L. Titius h(eres)ue eius
uellet pecunia praesenti uenderet ; mancipio pluris HS n(ummo) I
inuitus ne daret, neue satis secundum mancipium daret, neue
ut in ea uerba, quae in uerba satis s(ecundum) m(ancipium) dari
solet, repromitteret, neue simplam neue (*duplam*)...

q. *Lex* is probably connected rather with the root of *ligare* than with

that of *legere;* see Corssen Ausspr. 1², 444 and Curtius Grundzüge
173. Considered in connection with *mancipium, lex* and *nexum*
appear only to differ in so far as the latter is the bond or obligation between the parties, and the former the expression of it.

§ 23.

Testamenta calatis comitiis and per aes et libram.

The *testamenti factio per aes et libram,* being a form of
mancipation, naturally comes here, but the old form of will
which it superseded deserves a brief notice. *Arrogatio* could,
as we have seen (p. 28), be only performed at a meeting
of the Curies. The first wills were made at a ' summoned
meeting,' in the first instance doubtless of the same Curies.
The primary object of these 'Calata Comitia' would appear from Gellius* to be the inauguration of a rex or
flamen. As these were life offices, a meeting for the purpose of filling up a vacancy would be occasional and
specially summoned, which is probably the origin of the
name. So Macrobius makes the people to be summoned
by the pontifex minor to the Curia Calabra as soon as he
has caught sight of the new moon, whose rising, though
to us a tolerably regular event, was originally treated as one
to be specially observed for each individual occasion⁵.
However, at those Calata Comitia was also performed the
making of testaments and the *detestatio sacrorum*⁸. The
subject-matter with which the latter solemnity dealt is
clear: whether it was a formal notice to take up certain
sacra priuata or a formal disavowal of them is not clear*.
But there can, I think, be little doubt that the secondary
or incidental function of the Comitia Calata (which were
always held under the presidency of the pontiffs) was to

supervise the maintenance and proper devolution of the
sacra priuata. And when this business assumed, as we
shall shortly see that it did, a form which was in frequent
practical requisition, the incidental function of the Comitia
Calata might well become a substantive one, and lead to
their being held at regular intervals instead of being
merely called when a king or flamen died. Indeed, a
formerly questioned statement of Theophilus, that the
Calata Comitia took place regularly twice a year has been
confirmed by the discovery of Gaius' Commentaries[c].
Considering, then, the peculiar subject-matter with which
these Calata Comitia dealt, as also the antiquity implied
by that subject-matter, by their name and by the name of
the officer (not yet *rex sacrificulus,* but *rex*) with whose
inauguration they were originally concerned; it does not
seem too bold to identify them with those assemblies of
the Curies which transacted the business of arrogation
under the same presidency (of the pontiffs). The naming
of an heir being once allowed, more general powers of
disposing of an inheritance would naturally follow, the
supervision of the pontiffs providing for the perpetuation
of the *sacra,* and the meeting of burgesses, as Mr Maine
suggests, for the protection of the rights of the *gentiles.*

The assembly of the Curies, although perhaps not
exclusively patrician (see below, § 27, p. 137), would
certainly seem from the functions which it discharged
to have been essentially *gentile.* It was scarcely likely
that this venerable assembly would concern itself about
the last wishes of any one not a member of a *gens.*
But the Servian reform doubtless gave similar testamentary powers to any one on the census-roll. For the
words of Gellius on the subject of *Calata Comitia* clearly
shew that these meetings were called of the *centuries* as
well as of the Curies, a point which has been much over-

looked. The first wills, then, were oral declarations of the testator's wishes as to his inheritance, before an assembly of the people, in all probability formally *put* (*rogata*) like the arrogations from which they were derived, with the sanction of the pontiffs [d]. If we may be allowed to translate the custom into a modern form, every such will was a private act of parliament passed subject to the veto of the Episcopal Bench. The inconvenience and probable expense of such a system is evident in the case of either curies or centuries, but more in that of the centuries, as being the larger assembly: so that it may have been, (as is sometimes assumed,) by those who had to avail themselves of the *latter*, that the new form of will was devised. This was a legal transfer (*mancipatio*) of the inheritance *inter uiuos*, with that payment of a nominal consideration which seems to have been the first legal method of creating an obligation between parties. The perfectly *mutual* character of the *nexum* is seen here in the fact that it must have been the *payer* of this consideration, the 'purchaser of the family,' as he was called, who became bound to fulfil the 'binding direction (*lex*)' of the *mancipium*. The act of declaration by the testator (*nuncupatio*) originally perhaps stated his wishes in full, afterwards by reference to the tablets, which, from his calling the five witnesses to attest their delivery, became the 'tablets of his testament;' and lastly, by an easy change, the 'testament' itself that has descended to modern times. Gaius describes the whole ceremony in a well-known passage [e] in which the only points that appear to require special notice here are the following. The words of the *familiae emptor* or trustee (who was originally the *heres*, the principal *cestui-que-trust*, also) seem to contain a reference to the law of the Twelve Tables. He declares himself to receive the property 'whereby thou mayest

make a valid (or binding) will in pursuance of the public
law.' This public law I have little hesitation in identifying with that of the Twelve Tables, so called as distinguished from the private *lex* or declaration of a *mancipium*[f]. From the latter comes the word *legare*, appearing
in the enactment in question, and which, first meaning
simply to direct, afterwards signified to leave away from
the *heres*. The word *iure* I have ventured to understand
'in a valid (literally binding) manner,' on the authority of
the words, in the Twelve Tables, *ita ius esto,* (so be it
binding.) translated according to the only derivation at all
satisfactory of the difficult word *ius*[g]. I mention this reference to the Twelve Tables for the purpose of remarking
that it merely fixes the date of the formula in which it
occurs as subsequent to that code. The previous practice
of testamentary disposition may rather be inferred from
the words of the enactment itself, which substitutes the
authority of law for that of custom. If *legare* be rightly
connected with the *lex mancipi*, the word *legassit* in the
Twelve Tables proves an established custom of mancipa-
tory testation.

The declaration of the testator was called *nuncupatio*,
for *nuncupare* signifies, says Gaius, to name openly (*palam
nominare*)[a]. The latter part of the word, which is clearly
the same as in *mancupare*, has here no explanation. If
we may regard *mancupare* and *nuncupare* as originally
antithetical—the manual taking and the nominal taking—
we may see a peculiar propriety in the use of the latter
word, where a continuing *nexum* was intended, where certain services had yet to be performed, and the transaction
was, at least in one point of view, executory. This is the
case with the *familiae emptor* in the *testamentum per aes
et libram*, where, however, the word doubtless soon passed
altogether into the meaning of 'declaring' those executory

services which the testator was perhaps originally considered as 'nominally receiving[h].'

There is a considerable analogy between this Roman artifice of making a conveyance *inter uiuos* do duty for a will, and the English feoffment to use of the feoffor, for a similar purpose, before the statute of uses. The owner became thus enabled to devise the use where he could not have devised the legal estate, which became vested in the feoffee as the *familia* in the *emptor*[i]. Whether the *nexum* in the Roman case included a trust for the testator during the remainder of his life, like the use with us, we do not know: probably not, as this will was only made on the approach of death[k]. It may be observed that the nominal consideration which seems to have created the bond between the parties in Roman law, would have been fatal to the *resulting* use which our Court of Chancery only held to arise where *no* consideration passed.

a. Noctes Atticae 15. 27. In libro Laeli Felicis ad Q. Mucium primo scriptum est Labeonem scribere *calata* comitia esse quae pro collegio pontificum habentur aut regis (? sacrorum) aut flaminum inaugurandorum caussa, eorum autem alia esse curiata alia centuriata. curiata per lictorem curiatum *calari* id est conuocari centuriata per cornicinem. isdem comitiis quae calata appellari diximus et sacrorum detestatio et testamenta fieri solebant. tria enim genera testamentorum fuisse accepimus; unum quod calatis comitiis in populi contione fieret, alterum in procinctu cum uiri ad proelium faciendum in aciem uocabantur, tertium per familiae mancipationem cui aes et libra adhiberetur. The *sacrorum detestatio* mentioned here and in Noct. Att. 7. 12 was very probably a solemn renunciation of family *sacra* made before the *comitia calata* and with the sanction of the pontiffs. This sanction was, doubtless, often difficult to obtain; from which fact, as the burden of the *sacra* become more and respect for them less felt, arose the artifice of shifting this duty upon some slave emancipated for the purpose (Festus *Manumitti* (*bis*); *puri probi* &c.), or upon some man of straw (*senex coemptionalis*), who become liable to the duty of keeping up the *sacra* whether by nominally purchasing the inheritance or, as the prefix *co* would seem to indicate, by going through the ceremony of *coemption* (below, § 26) with an heiress so liable. Cic. pro Murena 12. 27. Compare to some extent our *common vouchee* in a recovery.

b. Satt. i. 15.

c. Gaius Comm. 2. 101.

d. The form of rogation in arrogation is given by Gellius Noctt. Att. 5. 19. As to the pontiffs' sanction see Cic. pro domo sua ad pontt. 13. 35. pontificibus bona caussa uisa est : approbauerunt.

e. Gaius Comm. 2. 104. qui facit, adhibitis sicut in ceteris mancipationibus quinque testibus ciuibus Romanis puberibus et libripende, postquam tabulas testamenti scripserit, mancipat alieni dicis gratia familiam suam, in qua re his uerbis familiae emptor utitur "*familiam pecuniamque tuam endo mandatam tutelam custodelamque meam [recipio eaque] quo tu iure testamentum facere possis secundum legem publicam hoc aere et,* ut quidam adiciunt, *aeneaque libra, esto mihi empta,*" deinde aere percutit libram idque aes dat testatori uelut preti loco. deinde testator tabulas testamenti tenens ita dicit "*haec ita ut in his tabulis cerisque scripta sunt ita do ita lego ita testor itaque uos, Quirites, testimonium mihi perhibetote.*" et hoc dicitur nuncupatio : nuncupare est enim palam nominare &c.

f. *Vti legassit super pecunia tutelaue suae rei ita ius esto.*

g. *Legare* is interpreted, on philological grounds, by Corssen as *bindenden Auftrag geben,* to give a binding charge or commission. Ausspr. 1². 444. *Ius* is traced by the same author to a root *iu* (binden). The stems springing from this root mostly indicate *connection* rather than *constraint,* but the former meaning is quite proper in the case of a valid *bond between parties. Ius,* it may be remembered, belonged to *civil* not *criminal* law. The word cannot come from *iubeo,* an assumption on which much now exploded metaphysical and juridical speculation has been founded.

h. This view of nuncupare is slightly supported by the following passage. Festus. *Nuncupata pecunia...uota nuncupata dicuntur quae Consules Praetores cum in prouinciam proficiscuntur faciunt* ...at Sautra, L. ii. de uerborum antiquitate, satis multis nuncupata colligit non de recto (Müller directo ? unnecessarily) nominata significare sed promissa et quasi testificata circumscripta recepta, quod etiam in uotis nuncupandis esse conuenientius.

Compare, besides manu-, usu-capio. For the etymology, there is not much more 'loss' than in homi(ni)cida. The intermediate *in* dropping, contact with the *c* changes *m* to *n*. For change of *o* to *u* compare contiuncula, &c. See Corssen Ausspr. 2². 577.

i. 1 Sand. Uses. Williams on Real Property, chaps. 8 and 10.

k. Gaius Comm. 2. 102. Qui neque calatis comitiis neque in procinctu testamentum fecerat, is *si subita morte* urgebatur amico
familiam suam mancipio dabat, &c.

§ 24.

Testamenta in procinctu.

An exceptional and not very valuable privilege of
testation was allowed to soldiers, without distinction of
order, on the eve of a battle[a]. The well-known expression *procinctus* would appear from Servius' explanation
to mean that the sort of plaid which formed the ordinary
Italian dress, instead of falling in a loose fold over the
breast, was thrown over the back, then brought tightly
round the front of the body and tied so as to form a
girdle[b]. *In procinctu*, then, means in fighting order, and
the will in question was made, as Gellius informs us,
'when the men were being called into line for battle'
(see above, § 23, n. *a*), or rather, perhaps, after formation
in line and during the brief delay of taking the auspices:
for Cicero distinctly connects the cessation of the latter
practice with the disuse of testaments *in procinctu*[c]. At
what time they came into legal recognition it is difficult
to say: but they very probably took their rise in the
Servian military organization. The coupling of the
epithet *procincta* with the well-known technical term
classis, speaks slightly in favour of this theory, though
there is nothing to prevent *classis* (a calling or summoning) having been used for *any* body of soldiers, independ-
ently of the Servian constitution[d]. The allowance, then,
of this practice may possibly have been coeval with power
to make a will in the *calata comitia* of the centuries; so

that it did not amount to the conferring of a new right upon the plebeians, but merely to the dispensation with forms otherwise necessary. This is clearly the view taken by Cicero, who speaks of the *testamentum in procinctu* as also dispensing with the forms of that *per aes et libram*[e].

Heineccius ingeniously suggests that these wills were held valid because made by implied vote of the people, assembled, here on the battle field, as, for the regular wills, in their *calata comitia*[f]. In this opinion he is followed by Ortolan[g].

The *form* was an oral declaration of the soldier's wish to his fellow-soldiers present[h]. It is probable that the testament was only valid in case of the testator's death in that particular battle[i].

Testamenta in procinctu, having fallen into disuse towards the close of the republican period[e], were replaced by the *testamentum militare* temporarily allowed by Julius Cæsar, Titus, Domitian, and Nerva, and placed on a footing of permanent authorization by Trajan[k]. A similar allowance has been made in most modern systems[l].

---

a. Gaius Comm. 2. 101. aut in procinctu (testamentum faciebant) id est cum belli caussa ad pugnam ibant ; procinctus est enim expeditus et armatus exercitus. alterum itaque in pace et in otio faciebant alterum in proelium exituri.

b. Servius on Virg. Aen. 7. 612. Gabinus cinctus est toga sic in tergum reiecta ut una eius lacinia reuocata hominem cingat, hoc autem uestimenti genere ueteres Latini cum necdum arma haberent praecinctis togis bellabant unde etiam milites *in procinctu* esse dicuntur.

c. Cic. de Nat. Deorum 2. 3. 9. Itaque maximae reipublicae partes, in his bella, quibus reipublicae salus continetur nullis auspiciis administrantur: nulla peremnia seruantur nulla ex acuminibus; *nulla cum uiri uocantur*, ex quo in procinctu testamenta perierunt. The italicised words are a certain emendation (founded on Gellius' cnm uiri...uocabantur § 23. n. *a*, above) of *nulli uiri uocantur* the MS. reading.

While the general was taking the auspices, (we are told by Sabidius on Virg. Aen. 10. 241,) interim ea mora utebantur qui testamenta in procinctu facere uolebant. This *mora*, though longer doubtless in duration, answers well in point of time to our poet's:—

'One moment while the trumpets blow.'

d. Festus. *Classis procincta exercitus instructus.* See too *Opima spolia, endo procinctu*, and *procincta*. Dionysius Antiqq. 4. 18. ἐγένοντο δὲ συμμορίαι μὲν ἓξ ἃς καλοῦσι Ῥωμαῖοι κλάσεις...ὃ γὰρ ἡμεῖς ῥῆμα προστακτικῶς σχηματίζοντες ἐκφέρομεν, κάλει, τοῦτ' ἐκεῖνοι λέγουσι κάλα, καὶ τὰς καλέσεις ἀρχαῖον ἐκάλουν κλάσεις. The explanation of κάλει is probably that the *name* of the Epsilon, which (as following the λ) corresponded to a Latin a, was not ε or η but ει (Roby's Latin Grammar, lxvii). The passage from Dionysius is rather in favour of a borrowing of classis from Doric Greek (which is Mommsen's theory) than of derivation from a stem cla-t (cf. Gothic la-th-ôn) by which Corssen proposes to account for the first κ. Ausspr. 1³. 490. Curtius Grundzüge 133. The meaning is the same in either case.

e. Cicero de Oratore 1. 53 § 228. tanquam in procinctu testamentum faceret sine libra et tabulis.

f. Heinecc. Antiqq. Syntagma 2. 10. 3.

g. Ortolan Explication § 651.

h. Festus. *In procinctu* factum testamentum dicitur quod miles pugnaturus nuncupat praesentibus commilitonibus.

i. Heinecc. Antiqq. Syntagma 2. 10. 4.

k. Digest. 29. 1. 1. pr. Militibus liberam testamenti factionem primus quidem Diuos Iulius Caesar concessit, sed ea concessio temporalis erat: postea uero primus Diuos Titus dedit; post hoc Domitianus; postea Diuos Nerua plenissimam indulgentiam in milites contulit eamque et Traianus secutus est et exinde mandatis inseri coepit caput tale &c. The gist of the 'caput' is 'ut quoquo modo testati fuissent rata esset eorum uoluntas.'

The above is due to Ulpian, who also in Frag. 23. 10 speaks to the same effect, adding, as to the duration of such wills, 'sed quod testamentum miles contra iuris regulam fecit ita demum nalet si uel in castris mortuos sit uel post missionem intra annum. Compare Gaius Comm. 2. 109—111. Justin. Instt. 2. 11, specially § 3.

l. 1 Vic. c. 26 § 11. Code Napoléon (Civil) Liv. 3. Tit. 2. Sec. 2. &c.

§ 25.

EMANCIPATIO. NOXAE DEDITIO. ADOPTIO.

CONSISTENTLY with the view that *ownership* was the main constituent element of *potestas*, we find the legal conveyance forming a large part of these acts in law by which that peculiar relation was transferred, modified or extinguished. Of these, the emancipation of a son from the father's power was in all probability recognized rather than created by the enactment of the Twelve Tables, 'if a father shall have thrice sold his son, let the son be free from the father[a]'. This practice, then, may have dated from shortly after the introduction of mancipation. There does not seem, however, any ground for supposing that the mancipation of a son was introduced merely for the purpose of setting him free. It was sometimes doubtless the bonâ fide transfer of a chattel, which, for instance, in the case (*noxalis caussa*) of making over bodily an offending son to the person injured as amends for the injury, clearly existed in the time of Gaius, though it had ceased in that of Justinian[b]. It need not be now discussed whether such a surrender (*noxae deditio*) was introduced by the Twelve Tables or, as seems more probable, existed before[c]: the barbarity of the practice, which may have extended even to the surrender of dead bodies[d], speaks for its antiquity. The *noxae deditio* is merely mentioned here as a proof of the lengths to which the exercise of *patria potestas* was actually carried. The child indeed, as Dionysius tells us, was in some respects worse off than the slave. On the former's attaining liberty in the hands of his new owner, the father's rights were revived. To these, at least in this particular respect, the law at last fixed, as we have seen, a limit which had probably been

previously recognized by custom. And a strict interpretation of the law introduced the curious anomaly of less
ceremonial sufficing for the enfranchisement of a daughter or grandchild than for that of a son*. The form of
emancipation resulting from this enactment may be easily
made out from Gaius' Commentaries, 1. 132, though there
are some lacunae in this section. The only thing requir-
ing notice is the position of the son after the third sale.
The father's peculiar rights are now extinguished, and the
former son is in the position of a slave to the Emptor.
If, therefore, on his enfranchisement it is intended that
his former father should occupy the position of patronus
to him, he must be resold to the father, and finally manumitted by him; whereas on the two former sales, either
manumission or resale by the purchaser would suffice
equally well*.

The word emancipatus, in the ordinary signification
under which it has just been considered, apparently means
mancipated *away*, i.e. out of the father's power. It is
however sometimes used even by the classical jurists, as
it is certainly by the writers of the Augustan and pre-
Augustan period, to express mere mancipation, very often
a voluntary sale of one's self. So Plautus *Bacchides*, I. 1.
59, Nunc ego mulier tibi me emancupo, and the fine
passage in Horace's *Epodes*, 9. 12, Romanus (eheu posteri
negabitis) Emancipatus feminae, &c. Lambinus, on the
latter, takes what seems to be the true view that *mancipare* was strictly proper of the buyer only, *emancipare*
being said of the seller*. It is therefore not surprising
to find the latter word used even in cases of adoption,
where it is not intended that the *filius-familias* shall pass
out of *patria potestas* altogether, but only out of that of
the natural into that of the adoptive father*. Adoption
may of course be as old as arrogation, but would seem

not to be so, from the state supervision, which was practically required, being of a purely civil character—whereas
that required in arrogation was at least in part religious—
and from the employment of *mancipation*. The person to
be adopted was thrice purchased by the adoptive from the
natural father, the last sale being followed or accompanied by a formal claim (*uindicatio*) on the part of the
former, and surrender in court (*in iure cessio*) on the part
of the latter[1].

a. *Si pater filium ter uenum duuit filius a patre liber esto.* Ulpian
   10. 1. duuit is Schöll's future perfect. (p. 85.)

b. Gaius Comm. 4. 75—81. It was a question whether three sales
   were required here as in 'voluntary mancipations' or one would
   suffice. Compare on the whole subject Iust. Instt. 4. 8, especially § 7; also below, note *d*.

c. Ulpian in Dig. 9. 4. 2. 1. See note *d*.

d. See the fragmentary section 81 of Gaius Comm. 4. Compare too
   Livy's story of the Samnites surrendering Brutulus' dead body to
   the Romans. (8. 39.) The same author makes out the resurrender
   to the Samnites of Sp. Postumius and the other guarantors of a
   peace (after their capture at the Caudine Forks), to be a *noxae
   deditio*. Livy 9. 10. A. Cornelius Aruina fetialis ita uerba fecit.
   "quandoque hisce homines iniussu populi Romani Quiritium foedus
   ictum iri spoponderunt atque ob eam rem noxam nocuerunt ...
   hosce homines uobis dedo." Schöll would here apparently read
   noxiam following Seruius on Aen. 1. 41. (*noxam.* pro noxiam. et
   hoc interest inter noxam et noxiam quod noxia culpa est id est
   peccatum, noxa autem poena. quidam noxa quae nocuit noxia id
   quod nocitum accipiunt). Flaccus makes *noxia* the damage done,
   noxa the fault or its penalty. Festus *noxia* (bis).

   Schöll, then, seems to interpret *noxae dedere* 'give up to punishment' (εἰς κόλασιν). Of all this I can only here say that the simpler form is the more likely to come near the meaning of the root
   noc—hurt; and that the MS. reading of the passage from Livy
   seems at least as good authority as the opinion of the Roman phi-
   lologers and jurists upon the original meaning of *noxa*, when they
   do not affect to quote any ancient fragment. In the passage from
   the Digest, 'si seruos furtum faxit noxiamue nocuit,' Haloandrus
   reads noxam.

e. Gaius Comm. 1. 132, 4.

f. Göschen on Gaius Comm. 1. 132.

g. Festus is ambiguous. *Emancipati* duobus modis intelliguntur aut ii qui ex patris iure exierunt aut ii qui aliorum fiunt domini quorum utrumque fit mancipatione. The second clause may mean voluntary sale of one's self, as in the case of Antony, put by Horace.

h. Cicero de Finibus 1. 7... seueritatem (Torquati) in eo filio...quem in adoptionem D. Silano emancipauerat.

i. Suetonius, Augustus 64. Caium et Lucium adoptauit domi (as opposed to *in iure*) per assem et libram emptos a patre Agrippa. So too Festus (at least according to Müller's additions, mainly following those of Ursinus). [Mancipatione adoptatur] ut patris sui heres e-[-sse desinat: sed eius qui adop-].tet tam heres est qua-[-msi ex eo natus esset &c.] Gellius 5. 19. adoptantur autem cum a parente in cuius potestate sunt tertia mancipatione in iure ceduntur atque ab eo qui adoptat apud eum apud quem legis actio est (= in iure, apud magistratum) uindicantur; adrogantur hi qui cum sui iuris sunt in alienam sese potestatem tradunt eiusque rei ipsi auctores fiunt.

Query, did the latter, after mancipation was introduced, employ that form, as the *nexi* doubtless did? This would give a good explanation of the expressions above cited from Plautus and Horace, as also of the second meaning of *emancipatus* in Festus (above, note *g*). For *uindicatio* and *in iure cessio* see above, § 19.

§ 26.

ORIGINAL LEGAL POSITION OF WOMEN AND ITS MODIFICATIONS.

WITH regard to the *patria potestas* the daughter was no doubt originally in no better position than the son. She might even be given up, according to the Institutes[a], like him, *in noxali causa* (see above, p. 125). For her marriage, of course the consent of those in whose 'power'[b] or tutelage she might be was necessary: nor are we surprised to find a form of *mancipation* employed for her purchase and sale, as a bride. This *coemptio* is probably, at least in the form we know of it, later than *confarreatio*, by which, however, it is quite possible that it was sometimes accompanied, as we now occasionally have a religious ceremony celebrated in addition to a civil marriage. *Coemptio* would perhaps be first used by those who had not family *sacra*, which were no doubt essential to *confarreatio*.

It may possibly have been from its originating among those with whom the paternal authority, though of course existing, was not a thing quite so sacred and supreme as with members of an old *gens*, that we do not in this marriage find it to be the father so much who sells his daughter, as the daughter who with his direction (*iussus*) sells herself[d]. *She* is generally said *coemptionem fucere*, and the compounded preposition is explained by Servius' view that this is a mutual transaction in which each party buys the other[e]. A *price* being apparently always mentioned, and the *aes et libra* being made by Servius essential to coemption, it does not seem necessary or proper here to have recourse to the original meaning (take) of *emere*[f].

The words which Boethius[g] makes the parties use in this marriage perhaps explain his strange statement that those who came into the husband's power (*manus*) by *coemption* were called *mater-familias* but not those who did the like by *confarreatio* or *usus*. These words are not unlike a modern form. They asked one another, the man, would she be his *mater-familias?*...and the woman, would he be her *pater-familias?* to which questions both answered, they would. The regular form of mancipation no doubt followed, and probably constituted the binding part of the transaction: indeed Boethius' account may be little more than a gloss upon the often-quoted formula, *ubi tu Gaius ibi ego Gaia*, words which seem according to Cicero to have caused the same trouble to the pedantic lawyers of his day as the mysterious letters *N.* or *M.* do sometimes to the catechumens of ours[h]. The statement as to *materfamilias* contained in this passage of Boethius is mentioned by Servius as an alternative theory together with what is no doubt the truer one—that *all* wives *in manu* were *matresfamilias*[i]. The other mode by which a woman passed *in manum* may be mentioned here, though all we know of its date is that it was in vogue before the Twelve Tables. I mean *usus* or prescription, by which cohabitation for a year, with the consent of those in whose power she was or of her guardian, transferred a woman into the power of him who was thenceforth her husband. This is merely an application of the wider doctrine referred to above (p. 110) and more particularly in the next section (p. 141).

Conuentio in manum, however, the technical term for passing into the power of a husband, was found undesirable by some persons, even in those early times, as it was almost universally avoided in later. Hence arose a practice of breaking the *usus* by a certain amount of absence during the year of prescription, which absence the law of the Twelve Tables fixed at three continuous nights[k].

The guardianship or tutelage exercised over women must be noticed here, as *coemptio* was also employed with reference to it, and it presumably existed prior to the Twelve Tables[l]. According to Roman common law a woman though of full age did not, like a man, become a perfectly free agent by the death of him in whose power she was. She merely passed into the *tutelage* either of a guardian appointed by the deceased or of those relatives, as guardians fixed by law, to whom on her death unmarried and intestate her property would come[m]. On these points the enactment of the Twelve Tables may with probability be considered as merely 'declaratory of the common law.' The special exception of the Vestal virgins contained in that code[n] sufficiently proves the rule, and the normal condition of all other women. So that even if a woman abstained from marriage or at least from those forms of marriage which brought her and all her property into the 'power (*manus*)' of a husband, her liberty to deal as she would with her own was of a most questionable kind.

She succeeded, it is true, to her share of property, but she could not, in the old times, alienate it, or perform any act in law whatever, without the sanction of her *tutor*, who might be an interested relative. 'To every act,' says Livy, 'even of a private character, done by a woman, our ancestors required the sanction of a *tutor*[o].' It is true that this rigid primitive law was in time evaded, and even overruled by equitable regulations proceeding from the state tribunals themselves. Gaius, curiously anticipating a now well-known argument, scouts the idea of a 'want of weight in the female mind' as forming any good reason for their state of wardship: 'because,' says he, 'women of full age manage their affairs for themselves, and in some cases the tutor puts in his sanction by way of form : nay, is often obliged to give it against his will by the praetor' (whom we may here perhaps identify with the Court of Chancery)[p]. Originally, however, a single woman on the death by which a man would have become perfectly free, had a tutor cast on her by law (if one had not been otherwise appointed for her), who was interested in the succession to her property, and without whose sanction she could neither alienate the portions of that property regarded as most valuable by the old law[q], nor make a will at all[r].

Down to the time of Gaius the statutory tutor could not be compelled to give his sanction to either of these acts, and that avowedly because of his own conflicting interests[a]. In fact until the passing of a *Senatus-con-sultum*, under Hadrian, not even the sanction of a *statutory* tutor would suffice to validate a woman's will, but she must first have come into the tutelage of a trustee by the cumbrous process of coemption, remancipation, and manumission. This point of law we see confirmed by a passage of Cicero[b]. The trustee or fiduciary tutors, of whom Cicero complains[c], were of course flexible enough, but it must be remembered that the sanction of the *statutory* tutor was necessary before a woman could effect the formal coemption through which she exchanged *his* tutelage for that of her own choice. The state of wardship with women was for life, not, as with males, terminable at puberty[d].

a. Iustin. Instt. 4. 8. 7.

b. Iustin. Instt. 1. 10. pr. dum tamen, si filii familias sint (here including daughters) consensum habeant parentium quorum in potestate sunt.

　　　Digest 23. 2. 2. Nuptiae consistere non possunt nisi consentiant omnes id est qui coeunt quorumque in potestate sunt.

　　　Ulpian Frag. 5. 2. Iustum matrimonium est si inter eos qui nuptias contrahunt conubium sit et tam masculus pubes quam femina uiripotens sit, et utrique consentiant si sui iuris sint aut etiam parentes eorum si in potestate sint.

c. Cicero pro Flacco 34 § 84 so far as regards *usus* and *coemptio.*

　　　In manum, inquit, conuenerat. nunc audio. sed quaero usu an coemptione? usu non potuit. nihil enim potest de tutela legitima nisi omnium tutorum auctoritate deminui. coemptione? ergo omnibus (tutoribus) auctoribus. See too Ulpian Frag. 11. 22, 27.

d. Heineccius however quotes an inscription,—PVBL. CLAVD. ' ' ANTONINAM VOLVMNIAM VIRGINEM VOLENT. AVSPIC. A PARENTIBVS SVIS COEMIT. ET. FAC. IIII. IN DOM. DVXIT. I do not know his authority. It was, doubtless, the independent, or at least concurrent, action of the daughter which constituted the difference, both in form and result, between c×emption and ordinary mancipation. See Gaius Comm. 1. 123.

e. Servius on Georg. 1. 31. Teque sibi generum Tethys emat omnibus undis. quod autem ait *emat* ad antiquom nuptiarum pertinet ritum quo se maritus et uxor inuicem emebant sicut habemus in iure. And on Aen. 4. 103. *liceat.* sane hic coemptionis speciem tangit. coemptio enim est ubi libra atque aes adhibetur et mulier atque uir in se quasi emptionem faciunt, &c. See his note also on 1. 211. *dominum.*

f. Festus. *Emere* quod nunc est mercari antiqui accipiebant pro sumere. Cf. adimere, perimere, &c.

g. Boethius in Topica 3. § 14. quae .. in manum per coemptionem conuenerant eae matres-familias nocabantur quae uero usu uel farreo minime. coemptio uero certis sollemnitatibus peragebatur et sese in coemendo inuicem interrogabant, uir ita: an sibi mulier mater-familias esse uellet? illa respondebat, uelle. item mulier interrogabat: an uir sibi pater-familias esse uellet? ille respondebat, uelle.

This commentator is the author of the celebrated work, translated by our own Alfred, De consolatione philosophiae. See the fine eulogium on him in Gibbon's 39th chapter. He was executed A.D. 526.

h. Cicero pro Muraena 12. § 27. Quia in alicuius libris exempli caussa id nomen inuenerunt, putarunt omnes mulieres quae coemptionem facerent ΘΑΙΑΣ uocari.

i. Seruius on Aen. 11. 476. *matronae.* See Cicero Topica 3. § 14, who there gives a tolerably crucial instance, Si ita Fabiae pecunia legata est a uiro, si ei uiro uxor mater-familias esset, si ea in manum non conuenerat nihil debetur. genus est uxor; eius duae formae: una matrum-familias, earum quae in manum conuenerunt; altera earum quae tantummodo uxores habentur.

Also Gellius Noctes Atticae 18. 6. Illud .. probabilius ... matrem-familias appellatam esse eam solam quae in mariti manu mancipioque aut in eius, in cuius maritus, manu mancipioque esset: quoniam non in matrimonium tantum sed in familiam quoque mariti et in sui heredis locum uenisset.

It is possible that the term *mater-familias* may have been laxly applied to a woman *sui iuris* and *un*married. See Ulpian in Digest 1. 6. 4. Patres-familias sunt qui sunt suae potestatis siue puberes siue impuberes; simili modo matres-familiarum. Also, though the following is not so clear, Frag. 4. 1. Sui iuris sunt familiarum suarum principes id est pater familiae itemque mater familiae. But the ordinary meaning of the term is clearly that given by Gellius and a statement sometimes quoted from Nonius (de compendiosa doctrina per litteras) is simply absurd. 'Ma-

trem-familias (esse nuncupatam) quae in familia mancipioque
sit patria etsi in mariti matrimonio esset.' Both this and the
statement of Boethius as to wives *usu uel farreo* (above, note *g*)
may have arisen from a consideration of the exceptional case
given in the mutilated § 136 of Gaius' first book, which must, I
think, really refer only to wives who passed *in manum* (by confarreation), *sacrorum caussa*. See Göschen on that passage. Also
Tacitus Ann. 4. 16.

k. Gaius Comm. 1. 111. Usu in manum conueniebat quae anno
continuo nupta perseuerabat; nam uelut annua possessione usu-
capiebatur in familiam uiri transibat filiaeque locum obtinebat.
itaque lege xii tabularum cautum erat si qua nollet eo modo in
manum mariti conuenire ut quotannis trinoctio abesset atque ita
usum cuiusque anni interrumperet; sed hoc totum ius partim
legibus sublatum est partim ipsa consuetudine oblitteratum est.
See Gellius 3. 2. 12—13, where this breaking of the use is expressed by the word usurpari said of the woman. From usum
rupere (Schöll 104) comes usu-ripare, and, when applied to one's
own case, the middle usurpari.

l. Gaius Comm. 1. 144. 145.

m. Id. 1. 156. quibus testamento tutor datus non sit iis ex lege xii
tabularum agnati sunt tutores. 157. Olim . . quantum ad legem
xii tabularum attinet etiam feminae agnatos habebant tutores.

For the identity of the *tutores legitimi* with the persons entitled on intestacy see Gaius Comm. 1. 164. 5. The relation of a
tutor in respect to his *pupil's property*—that of reversioner or ex-
pectant—must have had some awkward consequences from the
earliest times. As to later, see Persius 2. 12, 13. pupillumue
utinam quem proximus heres impello expungam!

As instance of the *act* (not *thought* merely) to which such
wishes were father, see Suet. Galb. 9, Juvenal 6. 629, &c.

n. Gaius Comm. 1. 145. loquimur autem exceptis uirginibus Ves-
talibus quas etiam ueteres in honorem sacerdoti liberas esse uoluerunt: itaque *etiam* lege xii tabularum cautum est.

o. Livy 34. 2. The sentiment is attributed to Cato (major) in his
defence of the Oppian law, 'majores nostri nullam ne priuatam
quidem rem agere feminas sine tutore auctore uoluerunt.'

p. Gaius Comm. 1. 190. So Cicero, speaking of the practical elusion,
in his time, of the restraints of tutelage, says: Mulieres omnes
propter infirmitatem consili maiores in tutorum potestate esse
uoluerunt: hi inuenerunt genera tutorum quae potestate mulierum
continerentur. pro Murena 12. 27.

q. Gaius Comm. 2. § 80. Nunc admonendi sumus neque feminam neque pupillum sine tutore auctore rem mancipi alienare posse ; nec mancipi uero feminam quidem posse pupillum non posse.

Neither could such property pass by *tradition* and *usus*. Gaius 2. § 47. Item mulieris quae in agnatorum tutela erat res mancipi usucapi non poterant : id ita lege xii tabularum cautum erat. It must be remembered that the Twelve Tables no doubt contained the first statutory notice of *usucapio*; so that the last-quoted enactment is probably not the imposition of a new restriction on women, but their exclusion from a new (statutory) power of alienation.

See too the sweeping final clause in the following passage of Ulpian (Frag. 11. 27). Tutoris auctoritas necessaria est mulieribus in his rebus : si lege aut legitimo iudicio agant, si se obligent, si ciuile negotium gerant, &c.

r. Gaius 2. 118. Obseruandum praeterea est ut, si mulier quae in tutela sit faciat testamentum, tutoris auctoritate facere debeat : alioquin inutiliter iure ciuili testatur. Ulpian Frag. 20. 15. Feminae post duodecimum annum aetatis testamenta facere possunt tutore auctore donec in tutela sunt.

If a woman happened to have no tutor (a very rare case) she must apply for one in order to make a will. Livy 39. 10. Quin eo processerat (Hispala, a freedwoman) ut post patroni mortem, quia in nullius manu erat, tutore a tribunis et praetore petito, cum testamentum faceret, unum Aebutium institueret heredem.

s. Gaius Comm. 1. 192.

t. Ib. § 115ᵃ. Olim etiam testamenti faciendi gratia fiduciaria fiebat coemptio. tunc enim non aliter feminae testamenti faciendi ius habebant, exceptis quibusdam personis, quam si coemptionem fecissent remancipataeque et manumissae fuissent. sed hanc necessitatem coemptionis faciendae ex auctoritate diui Hadriani senatus remisit.

Cicero (Topica 4. 18) makes a *capitis deminutio* essential, under praetorian law, to possession in accordance with a woman's testament. Si ea mulier testamentum fecit quae se capite nunquam deminuit non uidetur ex edicto praetoris secundum eas tabulas possessio dari.

This *capitis deminutio* was the result, not of the *conuentio in manum* by *coemption*, which only put the woman in the position of daughter to the *coemptionator*; but of the resale, here a *mancipatio* proper, to the *tutor fiduciarius*, by which she comes into the position of *slave* to the latter. See Gaius Comm. 1. § 123. Si tamen quaerat aliquis quare citra coemptionem feminae etiam mancipentur, ea quidem quae coemptionem facit...seruilem condicionem...mancipati mancipatacue scrucrum loco constituuntur. I give the reading of Göschen's edition which seems to me best. The meaning clearly is, 'The reason for women undergoing mancipation besides coemption is that by the latter they do not enter into servile condition, by the former they do.' If a woman in the position of *filia* were manumitted, it appears to have been held that her manumitter (and subsequent *tutor*) could not aid her to disappoint the *agnati*. She must, therefore, to gain free power of testation, enter into servile condition, on which the *manumitter* became by common law her *patronus*, and that *patronus*, by an analogous interpretation of the rule of the Twelve Tables about *agnati*, her *tutor fiduciarius*. See Gaius 1. § 165.

u. Gaius 1. §§ 144, 145. The exceptional privilege under the lex Iulia and Papia Poppaea, as that in favour of the Vestal virgins, proving the general rule. See too § 194.

§ 27.

Commencement of the Republic.

THE expulsion of the Tarquinii and abolition of royalty only come under notice here as causing change in legislation or judicature. Both appear to have been modified to a greater extent than we should gather from the words of Cicero in which he treats the consular authority as scarcely differing from the royal except in duration[a].

Whatever power of direct legislation may have been enjoyed or usurped by the Kings, it is clear that none such descended to the two first magistrates of the republic. The function of enacting public laws belonged to the *comitia centuriata*. It is possible that the older assembly (*curiata*) may for some time have retained a power of sanction or veto in matters of general legislation. But their sphere of action was undoubtedly soon confined to a few special departments, such as the passing of private bills (in the matter of arrogation), and the investiture of officers with military authority (*imperium*)[b]. The constitution of this assembly as of the *comitia centuriata* is a difficult and disputed question for which I must refer the reader to such histories as those of Niebuhr, Rubino, and Mommsen. A very able discussion of these matters will also be found in Mr Seeley's Historical Examination printed with the first book of his Livy. The conclusion at which I myself have arrived as to the *comitia curiata* has been briefly indicated already, i.e. that it was essentially a *gentile* assembly but was not exclusively a *patrician* one[c].

The legislative power of the *comitia centuriata* was probably at this epoch subjected to a constitutional check in the requirement that their enactments should be ratified by 'sanction of the fathers' (*auctoritate patrum*)[d]. It is clear, I think, that these *patres* are not identical with the curiate assembly[e]. They are considered by Mommsen as a convention of patricians distinct at once from the senate and the *comitia centuriata*, confronting the latter 'in firm and serried ranks like an Upper House.' In this view Mr Seeley appears to coincide[e]. With much deference to the two last-mentioned authorities, I am disposed to believe that the *patres* were, in this case, neither more nor less than the Senate, which we know to have borne that title and to have gradually appropriated to itself the different branches of power from the commencement of the republic till its decay[f].

The Senate was no doubt originally a body of advisers chosen by the consuls in the same manner as before by the kings; the choice being perfectly arbitrary, and therefore falling usually on intimates of the consuls for the time being. The power of removal was probably exercised but very rarely, and the chance of being left out on the general revision at the census came only every fourth year. Merit began to be recognised as a qualification for the Senatorship, at least after the institution of censors:

rejection became a direct stigma, and would therefore be
in general sparingly used[g]. Subject to the chances of
omission or rejection here mentioned, a senator's office
was for life: moreover the practice grew up of allowing,
as a matter of course, a quasi-senatorial position to those
who had held a magistracy, which position would necessarily involve a preference for, if not a right of, admission
to the rank of full senator[h]. These causes did not, of
course, all operate immediately on the abolition of the
life-monarchy : but, even then, the comparative permanence of the Senate, as against the yearly Consuls, must
have given the former a great increase of power.   So
these *patres* who, whether the Senate, a portion of the
Senate, or a patrician convention, had certainly little or
no definite function under the kings, now enjoyed the
important right of veto if no initiative. That this veto
was a substantial power may be inferred from the necessity, in later times, of passing the Publilian law which,
making the sanction *precedent* and a matter of course,
reduced it to a mere formality[i].

How far the Senate may have enjoyed any independent
legislative power in the early republican period is matter
of doubt. The *Senatus-Consulta* which have come down
to us *in extenso*, belong to a much later time. They appear in fact to have been decreed on the sole advice of
this body as taken by the consuls : in form they are
rather opinions given to the executive than independent
acts of the legislative authority[k].

With regard to the administration of justice, the treatment of crimes seems, as before, to demand first notice.
Here, that supreme and final jurisdiction which some at
least of the kings, whether legitimately or not, appear to
have possessed, was clearly done away with. One result
of the appointment of two magistrates with equal autho-

rity was that a citizen, aggrieved by the sentence of one, might obtain assistance (*auxilium*) by calling to his aid (*appellando*) the other : failing this, he could summon (*prouocare*) the magistrate or magistrates themselves before the supreme court of the people, there to maintain the impugned judgement. The latter right is expressed very strongly and clearly by Dionysius, who evidently considers it as extending to all penal sentences, for he includes the case of *fine* in addition to those mentioned by other authors, of death or scourging[1]. And both limitations of the consular authority may be gathered from the passage in which Livy speaks of the dictatorship—a temporary revival of kingly power, soon found necessary either in the national or aristocratic interest— as an authority under which there was none of the relief that might be sought from one *consul* against the sentence of the other, nor any appeal[m].

This right of appeal, then, which was probably, as has been seen above (§ 15), a disputed point under the regal authority, was, on the downfall of that authority, raised from the position of a questionable customary to that of a definite statutory rule[n]. It is quite possible that no express penalty was attached to its breach: the real sanction probably was the danger which a consul offending against the law would run, of impeachment, after his office had expired, for *unconstitutional conduct*, which seems a more satisfactory meaning than that of mere moral censure attributed by Livy to the phrase *improbe factum*[o].

From the character of the sanction, this law might no doubt sometimes be, as Livy intimates, a dead letter in the case of very powerful offenders : but its formal import, as of the similar succeeding enactments carried by that ' *People-courting* ' family to which the first is attributed, was doubtless to place the supreme criminal jurisdiction in the hands of the centuriate assembly[p]. It should not be forgotten that this limitation of the consular power only extended to the city and a mile round, beyond which space their absolute military authority began[q].

In point of *civil* judicature, the consuls succeeded to a considerable portion of the kingly power. 'Judge,' in fact, appears to have been their distinctive title in relation to the people when within the city walls. When therefore an array (*exercitus*) was to be ordered, whether for military or political purposes, the consul's officer first summoned the Quirites to the presence of the 'judges,' by which term the consuls must be meant[r]. We should not infer from this title either that the private *iudices* were as yet unknown (see above, § 21) or had been discontinued, but that the line between their functions and those of the public magistrate was not so sharply drawn as it is supposed to have been in the later time of *formulae*. With regard to derivational meaning, the word is as proper for the one as for the other: and the decision of the *iudex* was always given by him merely as the delegate and under the commission of the magistrate. Whether the latter became now *bound* to refer civil cases to a *iudex* (such reference having been previously optional) is not perhaps quite so clear as Mommsen (II. 8, p. 449 of tr.) seems to assume.

Neither in civil nor criminal cases do we find any general jurisdiction possessed by the *pontiffs*, under the republic. With their special cognizance of certain offences committed by religious persons we have not here to do. Any other judicial functions that the pontiffs may, in the earliest times, have possessed, must have been merged in the royal power before that was superseded by the consular, and clearly descended to the consuls, not to the original possessors. As, however, retaining the custody of legal forms and precedents, the sacred college doubtless continued, both in the later regal and early republican period, to exercise a great, if an indirect, influence upon the administration of justice, and thereby also upon a species of legislation.

By means of their civil decisions, the chief magistrates of the republic cannot but have introduced a great deal of judge-made or magisterial law[a]. This is generally treated as if it only commenced with the institution of the *praetor urbanus,* an assumption based, no doubt, upon the name (*ius praetorium*) by which these modifications and reforms of the strict original law were most generally known. But it must not be forgotten that the name of *praetor* was borne, long prior to that institution, by the two chief officers of the Roman republic[b]. The title under which we usually know them, probably derived from their function of taking counsel with the Senate[c], was later than the general appellation of ' leader,' whereby they, as perhaps also any chief magistrates, were originally called[d]. So that praetorian is simply magisterial law, and, as such, must have had some existence from the very earliest days of any regular enactment at all. For the first laws of an infant state are brief, crude, inflexible ; and it is seldom that any easily available machinery is provided for repeal or reform. In the meantime, owing to the increasing complications and refinements of a growing society, new cases must arise, not contemplated by the strict law, and calling for equitable modifications or free rules of interpretation, amounting to little short of new laws, into which they often become formally converted. Such is doubtless the history of *usus;* in the case of which we may infer, from enactments of the Twelve Tables, a prior statute declaring that mancipation

or surrender in court shall be the *only* title conferring
full ownership of certain classes of property, and a practice of the magistrates allowing such ownership to spring
out of *other* titles, when followed by a certain time of
possession. Such is probably the history of those limitations which the necessities of practice imported into the
originally simple and absolute *mancipium*, and of the
employment of *mancipium* so modified for the purpose of
private testation. Some judicial recognition no doubt
intervened between the hard rule of old law and the
later enactment that, according to the verbal declaration
of the mancipator, or, according to the direction concerning his property, of the testator, so should it be binding[*].
And as in the last-cited enactment of the Twelve Tables
we have an instance where powers considered too narrow
were extended, so have we in the subsequent history of
testation an instance where powers considered too extensive were narrowed, by the accretion of judicial decisions
which came to be known as Praetorian law[x]. These decisions and precedents of course assumed a greater degree
of permanence and authority when they began to be
codified into rules and 'declared forth' (*edicta*) by the
yearly magistrate as the principles of decision which were
to bind himself and his *iudices*: but the principle of
indirect judicial legislation must, I think, have been
established before the *praetor urbanus*, and may perhaps
account for the very small body of statutes which so long
sufficed the Roman people.

a. Cicero de Republica 2. 32. 56. Atque uti consules potestatem
haberent tempore duntaxat annuam genere ipso ac iure regiam.
See too Livy 2. 1.

b. Of the many passages which may be quoted as to the *lex curiata
de imperio* the following appear to me among the most interesting

and valuable. Cicero de Republica 2. §§ 25, 31, 33, 35, 38, ad di-
uersos 1. 9. 25. Livy 5. 46, 52: 9. 38: 26. 2.

c. The *comitia curiata* are undoubtedly treated by Livy as representing
the *populus*, under which title it is almost certain that he must
have included plebeians as well as patricians. Seeley pp. 68, 69.
There are, I may add, two important passages, cited above (note *b*),
to which I think Mr Seeley scarcely gives sufficient notice. Livy
5. 46. Accepto inde senatus decreto ut et comitiis curiatis reuo-
catus de exsilio iussu populi Camillus dictator extemplo diceretur
militesque haberent imperatorem quem uellent......lex curiata
lata est dictatorque absens dictus. The first sentence is somewhat
confused, but I think there is little doubt that Livy treats *iussu
populi* as equivalent to *lege curiata*.

Compare with this 26. 2. Principio eius anni cum de litteris
L. Marci referretur, res gestae magnificae senatui uisae: titulus
honoris (quod imperio non populi iussu non ex auctoritate patrum
dato propraetor senatui scripserat) magnam partem hominum
offendebat.

It appears pretty clearly from this latter passage that *auctoritas patrum* was something distinct from *populi iussus*, i.e. from
lex curiata.

d. Cicero de Republica 2. 32. 56. Quodque erat ad obtinendam
potentiam nobilium uel maximum uehementer id retinebatur,
populi comitia ne essent rata nisi ea patrum approbauisset auctoritas.

e. Mommsen Hist. 2. 1. pp. 265, 269 of tr. Seeley pp. 66, 67. See
next note (*f*).

f. Mommsen Hist. 2. 3. pp. 327, 328 of tr. Ortolan (Histoire § 178)
treats the *auctoritas patrum* as that of the senate. One would
certainly expect to find more definite accounts of the body (if not
the Senate), with which so important a power as this universal
veto was deposited, than the vague expressions of Dionysius in
2. 60 and 6. 90, and the *patricii* of Livy 6. 42. The last passage,
upon which Mr Seeley mainly relies, as proving these *patres* not
to be the Senate, runs as follows: Per ingentia certamina dictator senatusque uictus ut rogationes tribuniciae acciperentur; et
comitia consulum aduersa nobilitate habita, quibus L. Sextius de
plebe primus consul factus, et ne is quidem finis certaminum fuit
quia patricii se auctores futuros negabant, &c. Is it impossible or
inconsistent with the conduct of the aristocracy in this struggle,
that after the senate as a body had accepted the rogations and
allowed the elections to take place, the patrician majority of that
body should afterwards refuse to accept the result of those elections?

g. On the original constitution of the Senate Flaccus' testimony is valuable. *Praeteriti Senatores* quondam in opprobrio non **erant** quod, ut̓ reges sibi legebant sublegebantque quos in consilio publico haberent, ita post exactos eos consules quoque et tribuni militum consulari potestate coniunctissimos **sibi** quosque patriciorum et deinde plebeiorum legebant; donec Ouinia Tribunicia (sc. lex) interuenit, qua sanctum est ut censores ex omni ordine optimum quemque curiatim (Herschk *centuriatim*) in senatum legerent, quo factum est ut qui praeteriti essent et loco moti haberentur ignominiosi. On the question *when* this lex *Ouinia* was passed and when a note of censure was formally recorded against rejected Senators, see Livy 39. 42, and Drakenborch's very full note thereon.

h. Festus. *Senatores*...[adiicitur] 'quibusque in senatu sententiam dicere licet,' quia hi qui post lustrum conditum ex innioribus magistratum ceperunt, et in Senatu sententiam dicunt et non uocantur senatores antequam in senioribus sunt censi.

i. Livy 8. 12. ut legum quae comitiis centuriatis ferrentur ante initum suffragium, patres auctores fierent. In 1. 17 he says, referring to the *patres'* sanction given to the election of a king by the *populus*, Hodieque in legibus magistratibusque rogandis usurpatur idem ius, ui adempta: priusquam populus suffragium **ineat,** in incertum comitiorum euentum patres auctores fiunt.

k. See the commencement of the Senatus-Consultum de Bacchanalibus (568 A.V.C.) Q. Marcius L. f, Sp. Postumius L. f, cos. senatum consoluerunt n(onis) Octob. apud aedem Duelonai...De bacanalibus quei foideratei esent ita exdeicendum censuere, &c. Also that de philosophis et rhetoribus (593 A.V.C.). C. Fannio Strabone M. Valerio Messala cos. M. Pomponius praetor senatum consuluit... Quod uerba facta sunt de philosophis et de rhetoribus, de ea **re** ita censuerunt ut M. Pomponius praetor animaduerteret curaretque uti ei e republica fideque sua uideretur ut Romae ne essent. Here, certainly, the Senate seem to give an order to the Praetor, though only on his application. (I have taken these **two** documents from Brun's Fontes iuris Romani antiqui.)

l. Dionysius Antiqq. 5. 19. Ἐὰν τις ἄρχων Ῥωμαίων τινὰ ἀποκτείνειν ἢ μαστιγοῦν ἢ ζημιοῦν εἰς χρήματα θέλῃ, ἐξεῖναι τῷ ἰδιώτῃ προκαλεῖσθαι τὴν ἀρχὴν ἐπὶ τὴν τοῦ δήμου κρίσιν πάσχειν δ' ἐν τῷ μεταξὺ χρόνῳ μηδὲν ὑπὸ τῆς ἀρχῆς ἕως ἂν ὁ δῆμος ὑπὲρ αὐτοῦ ψηφίσηται. Compare Cicero de Republica 2. 31. 54. Idemque, in quo fuit Publicola maxime, legem ad populum tulit eam quae centuriatis comitiis prima lata est, ne quis magistratus ciuem Romanum aduersus prouocationem necaret neue uerberaret. Also Livy 10.

) (below, note o). On the probably later extension of this law to the case of heavy fines see Mommsen 2. 1. p. 259 tr.

m. Livy 2. 18. Neque enim, ut in consulibus, qui pari potestate essent, alterius auxilium, neque prouocatio erat.

n. Ortolan Histoire § 94.

o. Livy 10. 9. Porcia tamen lex sola pro tergo ciuium lata uidetur quod graui poena si quis uerberasset necassetue ciuem Romanum sanxit. Valeria lex, cum eum qui prouocasset uirgis caedi securique necari uetuisset, nihil ultra quam *improbe factum* adiecit. id, qui tum pudor hominum erat, uisum, credo, uinculum satis ualidum legis. Compare Cicero de Republica 2. 31. 54. Neque uero leges Porciae, quae tres sunt trium Porciorum, quicquam praeter sanctionem attulerunt noui.

p. This is indicated by the stories of the removal or lowering of the axes. Cicero de Republica 2. 31. 55. Itaque Publicola lege illa de prouocatione perlata statim secures de fascibus demi iussit. The same worthy, according to Livy, before the passing of the law 'summissis fascibus in contionem escendit.' 2. 7.

Valerius Maximus 4. 1. 1. Inuidiosum magistratus fastidium moderatione ad tolerabilem habitum deduxit, fasces securibus uacuefaciendo et in contione populo summittendo.

See too Dionysius quoted in the next note.

q. Livy 3. 20. ad Regillum lacum...omnes id iussuros quod consules uellent: neque enim prouocationem esse longius ab urbe mille passuum; et tribunos, si eo ueniant, in alia turba Quiritium subiectos fore consulari imperio.

Dionysius Antiqq. 5. 19. ἀφεῖλεν (ὁ Οὐαλέριος) ἀπὸ τῶν ῥάβδων τοὺς πελέκεις καὶ κατεστήσατο τοῖς μετ᾽ αὐτὸν ὑπάτοις ἔθος, ὃ καὶ μέχρι τῆς ἐμῆς διέμεινεν ἡλικίας, ὅταν ἔξωθεν τῆς πόλεως γένωνται χρῆσθαι τοῖς πελέκεσιν ἔνδον δὲ ταῖς ῥάβδοις κοσμεῖσθαι μόναις.

r. Varro de lingua Latina, 6. 88. In commentariis consularibus sic inueni: qui exercitum imperaturus erit accenso dicit hoc 'Calpurni, noca inlicium omnes Quirites huc ad me.' accensus dicit sic 'omnes Quirites inlicium uisite huc ad iudices.' 'C. Calpurni,' cos. dicit, 'noca ad conuentionem omnes Quirites huc ad me.' accensus dicit sic 'omnes Quirites ite ad conuentionem huc ad iudices.'

Corssen makes *licium* 'girding' and *inlicium* = in procinctum. He considers therefore the first summons to be a 'calling into equipment' or 'mobilizing' of the people. (Ausspr. 1². 494—498.)

A statement of Livy is *against* the consuls having been originally named *iudices*. In speaking of an interpretation of the lex Horatia, according to which the protection thereby given to the *plebeian iudices* was considered as extending **to the consuls also**—iudicem enim consulem appellari—he adds—quae refellitur interpretatio quod his temporibus **nondum** consulem iudicem sed praetorem appellari mos fuerit. **Livy 3. 55.**

Cicero de Legibus 3. 3. 8 can only, I think, be relied upon so far as to shew that at some time or other the consuls **were called** *iudices* as well as *praetors;* not, as Drakenborch (on **Livy loc. cit.**) gathers, that they were first called *praetors,* then *iudices,* lastly *consuls.*

s. See for this meaning of *ius honorarium* Iust. Instt. 1. 2. 7. 'quod qui honorem gerunt, id est magistratus, auctoritatem huic iuri dederunt. It is a generic term, applicable, in later days, to aediles' law as well as praetors'.

t. See Livy 3. 55 quoted in note *r.* Zonaras Annal. 7. 19. Τότε γὰρ (a.v.c. 305) λέγεται πρῶτον ὑπάτους αὐτοὺς προσαγορευθῆναι στρατηγοὺς καλουμένους τὸ πρότερον. Festus. *Praetoria porta* ... initio praetores erant qui nunc consules. See also next note.

u. Varro (apud Nonium 1. 91). Iidem dicebantur consules et praetores; quod praeirent populo praetores, quod consulerent senatum consules. Compare the senatus consulta above quoted (*k*), and Corssen Ausspr. 1². 446, 'from their conducting the consultations' of the Senate and popular assembly(?) or (2². 71) 'taking those bodies to counsel.'

v. See above, note *t,* as to the consuls; as to the more general application of the term Livy 7. 3. Lex uetusta est priscis litteris uerbisque scripta ut qui praetor maximus sit Idibus Septembribus clauom pangat .... M. Horatius consul ex lege templum Iouis optimi maximi dedicauit anno post reges exactos; a consulibus postea ad dictatores quia maius imperium erat sollemne claui figendi translatum est. So, on the occasion which introduces the subject, senatus dictatorem claui figendi caussa dici iussit. (a.v.c. 391.)

This fixing of the year-nail took place *after* the institution of the Praetor Urbanus (a.v.c. 387), so that there were then two Consuls and a Praetor proper—enough to justify the use of a superlative, whether indicating greatest age or greatest dignity (Festus, *Maximum Praetorem*). But Livy clearly refers the *lex* to an earlier time, whatever be made of the difficult ex lege . . dedicauit.

Now as between the two consuls (originally praetors) the term must have been *maior.* Compare Festus, *maiorem* consulem L. Caesar putat dici uel eum penes quem fasces sint uel eum qui prior factus sit. Praetorem autem maiorem, urbanum; minores ceteros. In the last case the term *maior* survived from a time when there were but *two* praetors proper to a time when the addition of more would have justified *maximus*.

The inevitable conclusion, I think, is that *praetor* was an old general term signifying commander, which, though applied to the two chief magistrates who succeeded the king, was by no means invented for them or understood to be confined to them.

w. Cum nexum faciet mancipiumqne, uti lingua nuncupassit ita ius esto. (Festus, *nuncupata pecunia*.) Vti legassit super pecunia tutelaue suae rei ita ius esto. Ulpian Fr. 11. 14.

x. Gaius Comm. 2. 123 and following sections.

INDEX.